Cotton, Cornbread, and Conversations

ISBN 0-86554-873-0
MUP/P252

© 2004 Mercer University Press
1400 Coleman Avenue
Macon, Georgia 31207

First Edition.

Book design by Burt & Burt Studio

All photography by Suzanne Lawler unless otherwise indicated
Author's photo on page 212 by Kim Smaha

∞The paper used in this publication meets the minimum requirements of American
National Standard for Information Sciences—Permanence of Paper for Printed
Library Materials, ANSI Z39.48-1992.

Library of Congress Cataloging-in-Publication Data

Lawler, Suzanne, 1968-
Cotton, cornbread, and conversations :
50 adventures in central Georgia / Suzanne Lawler.
p. cm.
Includes index.
ISBN 0-86554-873-0 (pbk. : alk. paper)
1. Georgia—Description and travel—Anecdotes. 2. Georgia--History,
Local—Anecdotes. 3. Georgia—Biography—Anecdotes. I. Title.

F286.6.L39 2004
917.5'804043—dc22

2004002830

Cotton, Cornbread, and Conversations

50 Adventures in Central Georgia

Suzanne Lawler

MERCER UNIVERSITY PRESS | MACON, GEORGIA | 2004

You don't have to go far to find an adventure.

This book is for people who have lived in Central Georgia for years but never wandered too far off the beaten path, or anyone just getting into the area who wants a couple of ideas to get acquainted to their new home. You can even use this book as a reference for when relatives come into town and you say to yourself "where should we go this weekend?"

The stories and adventures come from different roads, people I talked to on the street, billboards on the highway, articles in magazines, someone's friend of a friend—you get the idea. And of course the festivals hit every year on the calendar. I love talking to people and telling their stories. They all care deeply about what they're involved in; whether it's the guy who makes grit cakes in Forsyth, the woman serving up tea parties in Thomaston or Rednecks having some fun in Dublin. Some of the stories are quirky, some of the stories will touch your heart, but all of them will prove to be places you'll want to visit and friends you'll want to make.

This book started with a phone call. (Doesn't it always?) But I didn't pick up the phone, my news director from 13WMAZ, Dodie Cantrell made the call and for that I am eternally grateful. I also want to thank the television station for their patience, enthusiasm, and support for this entire project.

I've always wanted to put words on paper, maybe that's why I'm a journalist, but I also think it has to do with my grandfather's love of books. I remember when he would take my brother and me down to Haslems bookstore in downtown St. Petersburg and let us spend ten dollars apiece. I'll never forget his love and the old smell in that great cavernous bookstore. (Haslems is still alive and doing well in the sunshine state!) And speaking of family I must thank my parents for their support in this endeavor but more importantly for teaching me that anything is possible. It sounds like a cliché but it's true. And Mom and Dad don't worry, now that this is finished, I'll make a few more visits home!

Thanks to my partner in crime for accompanying me along on a good many of these adventures, Kim Smaha. I think she had fun going to visit the world's largest peach cobbler and events like the watermelon festival, she even turned out to be a good sport getting stuck in the cemetery! But her advice, questions, and extra hands turned out to be invaluable.

Thanks also to Cindy Hill for opening her office so I could wander in and ask an opinion or two, Angie and John Wright, Robert Kapusta Jr. Esq., and all of the great folks at Mercer University Press.

And thank you for plunking down money to buy this book! I hope it's something you'll treasure and take with you on some of the same journeys so you can ask your own questions of these folks and hear their stories firsthand.

CHAPTER 1

Farms and Fun

There is no doubt the land is important to Central Georgians. Cotton, peanuts, and peaches reign supreme but garden enthusiasts can find a few rare treasures nestled in the cloak of farmland. From herbs growing wild at Olive Forge farms to some plow boys taking folks back in time with mules, each journey is distinct yet down-home enough to get your hands a little dirty.

Gift Cabin

Daryl working in the shed.

Olive Forge Herb Farm

Daryl and Marsha Herron never quite grew out of the sixties. Just imagine two very intelligent hippie folks married for 44 years that love to talk and grow their herbs. "We are not travelers," said Daryl.

The homebodies have a cabin and some land in Hancock County. Granted, it's a little challenging to find and when you drive down the entryway dirt road with a pond nestled in the dense greenery you still may wonder if you've arrived at the right place. It appears like an oasis, an open area where plants thrive and the air smells like a tangy Mediterranean spice fest!

Daryl and Marsha have a main area covered by a giant white tent where the tender little plants wait for their next home but don't stop there. Walk around their spacious yard. It's a peaceful experience, with shady areas and a healthy host of frogs singing out (especially during mating season). The couple wants you to come inside their house, a rustic cabin where you'll find a gift store with everything from home-made pottery to herb cooking books.

If you have time ask for a tour of the house, although it comes with all the modern day amenities they don't have a bedroom. Every night they just lay out the blankets, most times on the back porch, and sleep under the stars. But cold nights chase them inside by the wood-burning stove. "We have slept on the floor (sleeping pad) for over 30 years," said Marsha "We call it a resting rug so we can sleep anywhere we wish."

It's just the kind of folks they are.

The couple started selling basil, tarragon, thyme, and 320 other varieties of plants back in 1994.

Since then they've needed to add three greenhouses to the place.

You'll find typical parsley but you'll also find peppers so hot that Daryl and Marsha haven't even found a use for them (that means HOT).

The names can sound exotic, Greek columnar basil or a Syrian herb mixture known as Za'atar.

Even if you don't get sappy over sage, or think tarragon is terrific go to the farm for a relaxing experience. It's like a forest oasis. They have garden benches, a pond with some outspoken amphibians that share their space with the gold-fish, and other critters to keep you company. "Some just like to stroll through the gardens to see our triumphs and our failures," said Daryl.

Ollie the deaf Australian blue heeler doesn't care what grows and what doesn't; her world is dominated by the throw of a pinecone. "Ollie Grace never met a stranger, she thinks everyone comes to see her," said Daryl.

Don't bet on the same kind of hospitality from Kitty Boy the cat, she'll probably just saunter by like most cats do.

Whatever your wants and needs in the way of herbs for culinary enjoyment, if you like to mash a little coneflower into Echinacea, check out Olive Forge farms, and don't forget to ask to see the back porch!

....

Logistics

Address: 161 Browns Crossing Road

From Macon take Gray Highway all the way into Gray and keep going. You'll come into Hancock County about fifteen minutes out of town. Look to your right for a sign that says *Browns Crossing* and hang a right. Go about two miles and you'll see the farm on the left. It's not well marked. You really have to look for it.

Daryl and Marsha usually stay home Thursday through Saturday 9-5 unless those days fall on a major holiday. They encourage you to give them a call before you stop by.

Phone: (478) 932-5737

Email: oliveforge@alltel.net

John looking over his garden.

Menu of flowers

Towaliga Nursery

I f you travel anywhere in the country you'll see thousands, even hundreds of thousands of nurseries. But one nursery in Monroe County has a special claim to fame—a good portion of the plants, perennials, and trees originated on Georgia soil.

John Atkinson has run Towaliga plants for six years, but his mom planted the groundwork for the business years and years ago.

"We'd go walking in the woods and she'd show me things," he said. "I'm sure she thought I'd never be interested in plants."

It took a while for the sprout to bloom. John didn't pick up the passion until he turned 50. But now he's full throttle, creating the same woodsy space he explored as a kid. "I'm a plant nerd," he said. "I want one of every plant—the good, the bad, and the ugly."

The ugly is hard to find, especially when this soft-spoken man starts weaving his tales about native Georgia plants.

"This one called Hearts a' Bursting, you see it has the red heart and out come these bright berries," he said.

He'll show you the American Beauty Berry and the Brown Jug. He'll tell tales about the Grancy Graybeard and warn you about the horsetail grass (it grows nonstop and will take over everything!), then he'll coax you to smell the Cumberland Rosemary.

It seems odd; these native Georgia plants didn't have southern names. "It takes its name from the people who found it," he said. I guess he should know, this guy is a sponge when it comes to greenery. He talks to other gardeners, reads books, and watches anything garden-related on TV. "You can go to your competitors and they'll talk to you about propagating" he said, "there are no secrets in the nursery trade."

Which means you can pick his brain all afternoon long. This is a green thumb that's come full circle, from a boy wandering the woods of Forsyth to a man wandering the country looking for the best stuff to sell in his nursery. And by the way, John's mom never got to see the nursery, but that's okay, he says. "I think she would enjoy coming here!"

Logistics

You can stop by Towaliga nurseries Thursday, Friday, or Saturday.

To get there just take the Riverside Drive exit 171 in Macon off Interstate 75. Once you get off the exit set your odometer and drive exactly fifteen miles heading north towards Monroe County.

You'll see Lake Juliette and Plant Scherer along the route.

The nursery will appear on your left just before you cross the bridge to the Towaliga River.

Peaches bagged and ready to go

Looking down the line

Lane Packing Shed

I t's a fact. Folks seem to love Georgia grown peaches. After all, the area is known as the peach state. But what the Lane family came to find out eleven years ago is that folks really like the experience of seeing the golden fruit come out of the fields and make its way into boxes.

That's the main attraction at Lane Packing. Just like the name suggests, packing is the name of the game.

But maybe I'm getting a little ahead of myself. The Lane packing company actually started out in 1908 when John David Duke began his business.

Now four generations later three brothers and a sister take care of the day-to-day operations, but they live with memories of the past. "We all got our indoctrination in the packing house," said Duke Lane. "My Dad hired the high school football coach, Coach Faircloth to run things in the summer." Back then in the early sixties, the boys of summer had a pecking order. Every rookie started out upstairs in the warm loft for 45 cents an hour. "The more luxurious jobs were downstairs for 65 cents an hour," said Duke. "You'd get to fill the boxes, put tops on boxes, and put them in the cooler."

Today, Duke sits in an air-conditioned office. The memorabilia on the wall is a cross between his peach heritage and his love of turkey hunting.

In 1990 with the business doing well, the family decided to put out a small fruit stand. This went well so in came a couple of picnic tables. Folks seemed to crowd around, so the place got a little bigger, and a little bigger after that.

Now they've got a tourist attraction as well as a packing plant. Visitors can climb the stairs and get a bird's eye view on the cat-walk, of seventy thousand pounds of fruit making its way through the belts everyday. To break it down more mathematically that's one hundred and fifty thousand peaches an hour going through the process. Duke says he "still walks the catwalk in wonderment." and so do other people. "It's intriguing to see how it's done," said Duke, "what it takes to get that peach in a box."

Kids stare in wonder while adults talk about how the whole process is a lot more intricate than they imagined. What seems to surprise folks is the dozens of workers who sit all day at the belts inspecting the fruit for flaws as it rolls by. From the giant washer to the beeps of the trailers moving in for more loads, people know this is the real thing. This is how things work.

"It's really neat to see how it's done," said 17-year-old Sarah Edmonson, "I've never known."

Seeing is one thing but tasting is another.

Folks sit out in the shade in gently rocking chairs eating mounds of homemade cobbler piled high with peach ice cream.

Charon and George Bacon sat at a table finishing off the remnants of their dessert, both opting for the peach ice cream. "Instead of having puree in it, it has real peaches," said Charan. They have a friend that told them they had to stop at Lane Packing for the tour and the treats. "I bought some peach butter, I can't wait to taste it," said Charan.

The peach cobbler is another big seller and like the packing shed the recipe comes with a story. "Just an old fashioned recipe my grandmother had," said Duke. "It's got that soft crust."

For those that want to peek and run you can get the goods to go along with every other peach thing under the sun, pickled peaches, peach bread, peach pie mix, peach portraits, and a *Passion of Peaches* cookbook. It sounds like something out of Forest Gump.

The produce and paraphernalia doesn't just include peaches (which you can buy or ship by the pound or by the case), when it's in season you can get pecans, asparagus, strawberries, tomatoes and peanuts. And for the gourmet lover, rows of homemade jellies and dressings stand at attention to go out the door.

So after reading this if you want to go out the door check out the directions below and have a bite of cobbler for me!

....

Logistics

Coming from Macon take I-75 south. Take exit 142 and hang a right off the ramp. The packing plant is about five miles down the road on the right. You can't miss it! They stay open every day of the week from seven in the morning until seven at night.
Phone: (478) 825-3592

Outside sign

Scales in the shed

Skipper Farms

S kipper farms is the kind of place where you drive in to grab fresh produce or you walk the fields looking to pick a piece of nostalgia from the past.

It all started back in 1912. "My Granddaddy built it for my Dad as a wedding present," said Douglas Skipper.

The big white house came with ninety acres of land and that land has been producing okra, corn, blueberries, squash, and butterbeans ever since. But even with all the produce the Skippers didn't think about selling it until their son wanted to earn a little cash. "He wanted a three wheeler so he had to earn money," said Harriet Skipper. "We planted an acre, he picked the corn, sat under that tree, and sold out in two hours. The next year he sold double, finally got up enough money for a four wheeler."

And for 25 years after that the Skippers set up shop season to season selling out of the shed and letting folks roam their fields.

"We have some old timers that want to pick their own," said Harriet.

Gail Cox pulled in the dirt drive; she was in town visiting her daughter up the road. "I look forward to coming every summer," she said. "I know everything is fresh right from the field and you get to pick it yourself. I'd love to live three or four doors down."

Fresh picked corn

Don't be so sure, you might be growing for Douglas. His neighbor brings over buckets of "better boys" tomatoes that he sells for under a dollar a pound.

But the Skippers have scaled back the last few years. They say it would be nice to actually take a summer vacation. Don't frown, you can still motor up the driveway and talk to Douglas and Harriet for one month out of the year. They'll weigh your stuff and let you pet the llama and the miniature horses June 1 through July 1.

Just think of it as a time to act like a child, running through the blueberry fields, and searching for the next sweet treat.

Logistics

Open: June 1st-July 1st

Directions: From Macon head down I-75 to Hartley Bridge road and head East. Hang a right on Skipperton road and go on down to the stop sign. Turn left and the farm is on your right.

The Skippers have greatly reduced their operations. These days they're only selling a few items.

Plants spill over into the entrance

Garden cats waiting for a new home

Society Gardener

Nestled between two brick buildings, on what once was an abandoned concrete slab, is a very special nursery. It's called the Society Gardener. It's a place where decorative dancing fairies mingle with stoic iron fences, brightly colored Mediterranean pots lay on their sides looking at aged and worn urns, and metal daisies wrapped around gazing balls sit upright in pots of ivy.

Jackie Waters (pretty ironic) owns and runs the place. It's not something she grew into easily.

"I was a seventh grade science teacher for 20 years, but after awhile I just wasn't sparkly," she said. "And if I can't be dynamic I'm just not gonna do it."

She packed up and went down to Central America for awhile to think about the next stage of her life. On a return trip to Macon to visit her sick dad, she stopped into the

Society Gardener. Some friends of hers ran it and asked her to help out.

"I said okay but I'm not going to *talk* to anyone!"

Days have changed since she wound up with the deed. She talks to everyone while flanked by her dog Cuto, which in Belize means no tail.

Jackie has created a peaceful refuge with classical music flowing throughout the walkways and lush green plants bordering the aisles. But her soul isn't into selling.

"I'm not one of these ladies who likes to shop. I'll wear the same clothes until they rot off. It's kind of weird I ended up with this," she says.

Maybe it's not weird at all because she comes to work every day setting out to make the world just a little bit nicer.

"Basically we took a vacant lot, trash cans, litter and turned it into something beautiful and viable, so I think that's a good thing to do for a community," she said.

It is beautiful but if you have a mischievous side you might want to take a peek.

"I like funky crazy," Jackie says with a smile. "But Macon is conservative so I combine plant material with all kinds of stuff."

So if you want some Cuban oregano or just some time to yourself to relax, stop in and say hey to Jackie, but don't expect her to sit and talk all afternoon!

Logistics

Location: The Society Gardener is located in Macon, Georgia at 2389-B Ingleside Avenue.

Directions: Take I-75 to Pierce Avenue exit 167. When you exit turn left onto Riverside Drive. Take Riverside Drive to the light at Ingleside Avenue. Turn right onto Ingleside Avenue. Go through the first traffic light. Look for The Society Gardener on your right.

Hours: Monday through Saturday, 10:00 a.m.-5:30 p.m.

Phone: (478) 744-2402

If you get a chance, stop by in December. Jackie brings in reindeer and camels for the holidays!

Inquisitive Owl

Otter on the banks

Dauset Trails Nature Center

You'll never see billboard advertising for Dauset Trails Nature Center. "I like for people to come across it accidentally I want the discovery part to be accidental." Ike English sits back in his rocker on a large sprawling wooden front porch. He's the guy who runs the place. He grew up on a farm in South Georgia. After college Dauset Trails was his first job. A job he loves so much he wants to retire here. But his success with the twelve hundred acre nature center hasn't come from his marketing campaigns. "The biggest response we get is, 'I didn't know it was here,'" he said.

"The reason it's here in Central Georgia is to rescue and rehab injured animals. A good many become permanent residents. You'll see otters playing around in the pond (they beg for otter chow you can throw in for a quarter!) The two black bears have lived their entire lives at Dauset Trails. Born in captivity their mom was considered a nuisance bear in north Georgia. The Audubon society donated the bald eagle. Seems the bird had a run in with a car and didn't win. But maybe the most talked about animal on the trail is the two cougars. They have roomy cages, but you can get so close to them you'll hear the deep guttural purring as they walk back and forth swinging their lanky powerful tails from side to side."

"We got the second Cougar this summer. Someone in Georgia had it as a pet," explained English. "The cougars will never go back into the wild because they have no fear of humans."

But English's goal is to get the healthy animals back into the woods. "Yesterday we released a screech owl. We felt like it could survive on its own."

If English had his way he'd get all the birds and mammals back to their completely natural surroundings. "I wish there were no animals here. That would tell me man is doing a better job."

It's interesting to walk the trails accompanied by quite a few squirrels and chipmunks helping to lead the way. Say hi to the Red Fox. The Osprey will look at you with questioning eyes while the Buffalo just wander through the fields munching on their fibrous green diet.

Dauset Trails is much more than the cute critters. "The main thing they come out to see is the animals, then they find out about other things we have—miles of hiking and separate mountain biking trails. One guy came up to me the other day and said, 'I got lost' and I asked him, 'Did you have fun?'" Kids also have a special footpath to follow. It's an enchanted trail full of happy and creative garden art and places for kids to play, like a tea cup table (after all tea tastes tastier under the shade of big trees.)

So go on out and walk around Dauset Trails. It's a rare opportunity to connect with nature and meet animals you may only see in books.

Logistics

Dauset trails is open Monday 9-5 and Saturday 12-5. Ike and his crew take vacation Thanksgiving Day and December 25th - January 1st. Directions are found on the website.

Phone: (770) 775-6798

Website: www.dausettrails.com

Pat and Steve talk
to one of their birds

Proud Emu!

Misty Oaks Farm

Whedn Pat and Steve walked down the aisle thirty-six years ago they both knew they'd retire back on the farm in Macon. But they couldn't have foreseen what the crop would entail! On any given day around fifty emus and a few ostriches call the place home.

Just a quick biology lesson: emus stand in the Ostrich family. The ostrich in one of the largest birds in the world followed by their only slightly smaller cousin the emu. They're not the prettiest creatures and actually you've got to chuckle when they run around with their oval shaped bodies perched on long pole like legs. But as Pat so aptly put it, "All animals are kind of funny looking if you think about it." Point well taken!

The Jacksons's son got them into the bird business. He saw up in Pennsylvania where folks could bring in good money with emus.

So Pat and Steve started looking around. Then in 1992 they bought their first breeders. "We paid two thousand dollars a piece for them. We got a real deal and since then we've never bought another one." That's because as Pat explained, emus are pretty efficient when it comes to populating their herds. In the breeding season Pat or Steve will pluck out beautiful large grainy turquoise emu eggs. "They look like avocados to me," she said. And gigantic ostrich eggs. Some hatch out with little birds but a good many of them wind up on the table. In true Fred Flintstone style Pat explained to me how you can cook up one of these giants for breakfast. "Well you drill a hole in the bottom of it to get it all out," she said. "One ostrich egg is the equivalent of 12 chicken eggs and one emu egg is about six chicken eggs!" "People love them they come back for more."

And they also come back for the large array of emu products Pat keeps stocked in the store. The birds have a good bit of oil around their feathers. So when a bird is processed (they don't like to say slaughtered) they can get hand lotion, bath gel, and soaps. "I had a lady call me up at ten o clock at night and she wanted emu pills." Pat says the pills provide pain relief.

Pat and Steve will be happy to share their favorite emu meat recipes. Steve's vote is for the country fried steak while Pat loves to whip up a big old emu casserole. The phrase "tastes like chicken doesn't ring true in this case. It tastes like beef, not a wild taste at all," said Pat while holding up the emu cookbook that's for sale.

You don't have to buy anything to just go out and see all the animals. The birds hold center stage but Steve loves animals so Misty Oaks got a lot bigger. "Pat knows if she sees my truck pull in and I haven't come into the house yet I'm out talking to the donkey," said Steve.

The donkey shares land with the turtles, the goats, the chickens, a rabbit, a pony, and a dog.

I asked the couple if they take any ribbing about farming emus. Steve said sometimes the guys down where he works his day job jab him a bit but Pat has a different outlook. "We don't think it's crazy. We love it. We feed them, clean their pens, and that's it." And that sounds like a ringing emu endorsement!

....

Logistics

You can take a tour of the farm at Misty Oaks. You can stop by anytime as long as you call ahead to make an appointment with Pat. They also offer more organized tours for seniors and kids. On those jaunts folks get to taste emu snacks and make an emu craft. Just stopping by is free but there is a small fee for the organized tours.

Phone: Toll free 1-866-3EMU-OIL

Local: 478 781-1468

Email address: Theoil4u@aol.com

Directions: From Macon travel south on Interstate 75 to the Hartley Bridge road exit (it's just outside of town). Hang a left off the interstate and a right on Skipper Road, which dead ends to a stop sign, make a right on Sardis Church Road. Turn left on Nowell Road, go around the curve and you'll see the sign for the farm on the right.

Special Events: Every first weekend in May the Jacksons have an open house. They cook up a big pot of emu chili and have all types of activities at Misty Oaks.

Berry ready for picking!

Elliott Farms: Strawberries

Some of the first signs of spring present themselves in bright, red seeded, juicy little packages. While some folks get their strawberries from the local grocery store a lot of adventurous souls head out to the fields to pick their own fruit! They have a lot to choose from at Elliott Farms. The family has two fields with 80 thousand plants.

"You can get a pound of berries from each plant," explains Debra Elliott. She should know, she and her husband Russ baby the plants throughout the winter until they're ready to pop with the seedy fruit. Frozen temperatures spell a death sentence for strawberries. "We have a lot of sleepless nights in March. We set the alarm clock to go off at 37 degrees, said Debra. I have had the paper guy hollering 'what are you doing?'"

Their vigilance pays off the first of April. That's when folks start to show up for the pickings.

"Yup those are city folks," Debra decides as two ladies pull up and one of them immediately starts changing her shoes. Debra walks out to greet them, "y'all ready to do some pickin' today?" Rhonda Moody may come from the city, but she knows a farming philosophy when she comes to Elliott's. "We always have to taste as we go along to make sure they're good. It doesn't matter if they have a little bit of dirt on them." Her friend Katherine Maddox compares the experience to hunting for Easter eggs. "We like the strawberries to be looking for us, not us looking for them," she said.

Who knows if a berry will jump out at you, but Debra is used to folks asking all kinds of questions and making all kinds of comments.

"They want to know how we plant them and kids will run right around and go for the biggest berries," she said. "I say, okay stick out your tongue to see who ate the most."

They don't charge for tastes and the expert advice comes free too. "The burgundy berries are the sweetest ones. If you pick the green ones they'll turn red but they won't turn any sweeter," Debra explained. And to keep your own crop looking good on the table Debra has an inside tip. "Do not wash them before you put them in the refrigerator. Put them in an airtight container. That's the number one mistake people make!"

Even if, and this is unthinkable, but if you don't like strawberries, visit Elliott farms for the setting. You'll find the place down a dirt road, and when you get there, everything from peacocks to the family cat will walk up and say hello. Comfortable chairs sit around the edge of the fields, encouraging you to sit and chat for awhile. "People will say 'oh, it's like a whole different place' and they ask us if we have a cabin they can rent. Old timers like to sit around by the tractors and say 'I used to pick berries when I was a little boy for five cents a quart.'"

You can bet the five cents quart days have come and gone, but as for the Elliotts, they'll keep getting up on those winter nights to insure there are strawberries in the field. "We'll probably be doing this until we croak!"

Logistics

Directions: Off I-475 at US 80 to Lizella, then just follow the signs.

Hours: In strawberry season, April and May the farm is open 8 a.m. until 8 p.m., seven days a week.

Phone: (478) 935-8180

Price: In 2003, a pound you pick will cost $1.35. Debra says, they try to keep the prices cheaper than the grocery store. But in a store you'll invariably get a bad berry or two. At the farm what you pick is up to you.

Extras: You don't *have* to pick the fruit yourself, they also sell it pre-picked. They also have strawberry jams and syrups, ice cream, and other fresh produce for sale.

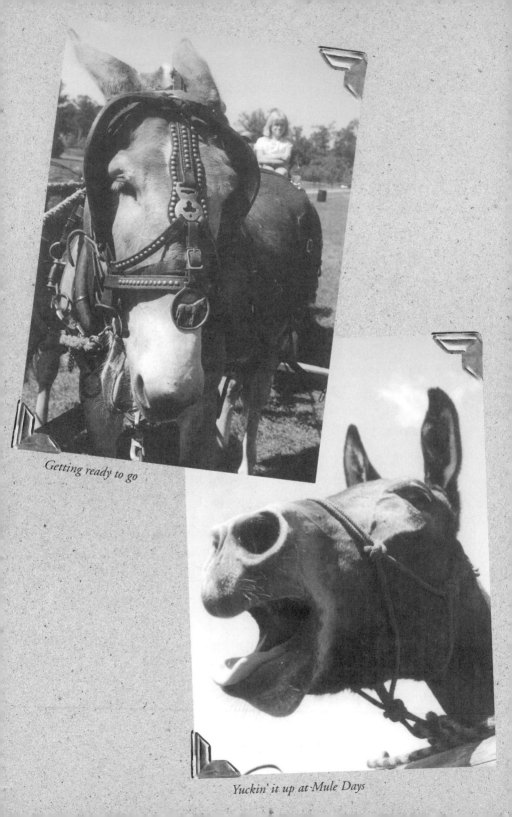

Getting ready to go

Yuckin' it up at Mule Days

Mule Days

You may have heard of such big name horse races such as the Kentucky Derby or the premier sporting events that trot out the best the thoroughbred world has to offer. Then there's a little event that falls the last weekend of April that brings out the most stubborn creatures central Georgia has to offer—Mule Days!

"I remember when I was 12-17 years old begging my daddy to stay out of school and plow his mules. He let me every once in awhile," Steve Montgomery said with a grin.

Now the 59-year-old doesn't have to beg to work the land he grew up on. He owns the family farm—four mules and about 200 plows to go along with the crews. "When the kids grew up I needed some pastime. I always liked old antiques and stuff and I don't care to fish or hunt."

Steve took his hobby one step further when he created Mule Days. "People laugh and say what in the world is a Mule Day? They say, you must be crazy or something!"

Don't feel like you're crazy to go, after all you get an up-close and personal look at plowing—how it looks, how it feels, and how it smells! Sure you've got the aromatic four legged animals walking around but you've also got that great green scent filtering through the air, kind of like after you mow the lawn but deeper and mustier. As the guys plod along you'll hear them murmur words to the hefty haulers like Gee and Haw! It's their own language but to translate, Gee means hey you head to the right and as you might have guessed Haw isn't a joke. It's a command to turn left.

Steve says the mule is pretty darn smart and it doesn't take too long for them to pick up the commands. He wants folks to know the mule is a lot more than just an ass. So now once a year, folks dressed in Bermuda shorts and decked out with 35 millimeter cameras mingle with old timers dressed in overalls with knowledge from the past.

You'll see SUV's and mule drawn carriages riding down the same dirt roads. Steve says the drastic differences show why there's a need for his event. "I know we couldn't go back to this, but people ought to know what their ancestors went through. Kids think most meat comes from the Piggly Wiggly."

Well those same kids get hands on lessons as they grab onto the gear to ride the plows through dusty dirt. Then for adults and kids the judges grade on form and the straightest lines. Eight-year-old Jessie Chastain gave it a go, her only experience with this kind of thing was riding on a tractor. She did a good job with a little help from Steve but don't expect this kid to beg for another chance. "It's scary. I got mud in my shoes." Yeah, that does come with the territory. It's funny though, even though folks come from five states to plow up to ten acres over a couple of days, the professionals won't take on each other for a trophy. "You don't do competitions with mule people," explained Steve. "They're real sensitive to that. Non-mule people are okay, but a man with a small mule is just as proud as a man with a big mule. We don't want to insult anybody." Sounds like there's a little stubbornness to go around!

Logistics

When: Mule Days is in Taylor County, Georgia, during the last weekend in April.
Phone: (478) 847-4270 (this is Steve's barn phone so you may have to leave a message!)

Water bubbling from the spring

The spaceship well

Indian Springs

When you drive into Indian Springs State Park you might think it's just like every other state park in the land. Set in a woodsy background, it has trails, a fishing lake, a pioneer campground complete with cottages (for those who really don't want to rough it), a putt putt course, and of course picnic shelters. But one of its claims to fame is its history—it's the oldest state park in the nation!

If you go back in history to 1825, Chief William McIntosh of the Creek Indians and some of his crew signed the Treaty of Indian Springs. In that document the chief sold the land for twenty-five thousand bucks. At the time it wasn't the wisest thing for the Chief to do. The chief of the Upper Creeks stood outside and yelled death threats to McIntosh. It seems it stood as a Creek law saying it was illegal to sell any more land. Three months after the signing Creek Indians killed McIntosh thinking that he took a bribe for the deal.

But a deal is a deal and as time went on the town of Indian Springs grew and flourished. Builders put up many famous resorts, one of them still stands as a remodeled structure named after McIntosh.

Now since the deal happened in 1825 the public had access to the land's mineral spring, even though Georgia's state park system didn't develop until 1926. History logs this as the oldest park because of the free access to the water.

Granted, not many people can tell you about the history, but folks line up and come from all over to get some of the water. It's free; all you have to do is bring some sort of a container to catch the liquid that runs out of the earth. As I met Doris Hardy she was busy urging her teenage grandson up the trail to get in line with their twelve gallon jugs! "It tastes soft and mellow like going down" she said, "about 70 years ago, when I was a child it was just a hole in the rocks." Technically it's still a hole in the rocks, but that hole is covered by a big glass see through space ship looking hood that covers the area and the water flows out of a silver faucet, making the whole process a little easier to fill up! It runs all the time never stopping, drains catch the excess. The shady stone covered shed where you get the stuff does have a distinct odor about it, like rotten eggs. Apparently it takes awhile for that color to wear off. "I have to let the smell out for a couple of days before I drink it" explained La Bragg. She traveled two hours from Dallas, Georgia to scoop up the water. "My nephew has asthma. When he drinks it, it goes away," said Bragg. And despite the smell it may be that medicinal legend that brings folks to the watering hole.

"One lady came back and forth from California. She finally moved to Georgia just to be around the water. She said it's keeping her alive." Christina Barber's worked as a ranger at the park for a couple of years now and she's heard all kinds of stories about the wet stuff. "You hear all kinds of testimonials. One man brought his wife with cancer and wanted to know my honest opinion on the water. I told him it can't hurt, just look at all the minerals in it." The breakdown of minerals hangs right over the well and the culprit of the smell may lie in the fact that sulfur tops the list at 24 percent. I cupped my hands together and tried the stuff. It reminded me of the sulfur filled water we'd make fun of at summer camp in Florida. As for Barber she didn't care for it either. "It's nasty, I didn't like it. My husband said hey since you work there why don't you bring some of that water home. It messed up his stomach for a week and after that he said don't get anymore of that water!" But for believers like Doris and thousands like her, the old Indian water surrounded by the long history is the best around. "I don't know if it keeps you younger, but it sure is good on your kidneys!"

Logistics

Directions: From Macon take I-75 northbound towards Atlanta. Just outside of Forsyth take exit 188. Hang a right off the ramp and about 20 minutes up the road you'll see the tiny town and the state park on the left. The water shed is down Sulfur Springs Road in the park.
Hours: Christina says folks are lined up to get the water at seven in the morning and the Rangers have to run folks off at seven at night when they close.
Phone: (770) 504-2277
Website: gastateparks.org

*Ray
uncorking
a bottle*

Tool shed in the vineyard

Courson's Winery

To get to wine country in Napa Valley California you would have to travel 2,581.17 miles. Or you could opt for a closer journey to Sparta, Georgia. Yes, Sparta. You can tell that you're close to the home grown vineyard when you see an old wooden hand painted sign on the side of the road that says Courson's Winery. Okay it's not fancy high-class advertising but consider the source of the winery. Raymond "Bo" Courson creates his fine beverage inside a tool shed!

"I know for a fact we're the smallest winery in the state of Georgia and I think we're the second smallest in the United States," Bo says with a grin. His numbers might be right on, after all the guy only has 1000 gallon capacity and Bo does boast it's a bare bones operation. But before you turn up your nose thinking this is just some yahoo in a t-shirt grinding out grapes in the woods, consider this: Bo goes by federal regulations and he's got the health guys in checking out his operation. And even though it all happens in a tool shed, it's a specifically designed 12x28 very clean tool shed. Inside he's got big see through jugs of wine aging on the shelf with little red plastic air locks sitting on top. Fifty-five drums of fermenting fruit give off that winery flavor to the place. By the way, Bo doesn't use his feet to smash the fruit, that would be scary! "I think the health department would get upset about that." But Bo is a country boy and he has had to make use of the finer tools of the trade, like a boat oar to stir around the crop! "Everything I do by hand, there's no mechanism."

The winery is his baby, but he does get help bringing in all the fruit it takes to make the stuff. Courson's winery sits right in front of a field full of 1000 muscadine vines. Bo also grows blackberries. Those flavors make up the crux of his crop but he's also experimented with apple and peach wines. "At its basic level wine is just fruit and yeast. I guess you could make it out of poison ivy but who would drink it?" Interesting point! Anyway, for ten dollars a bottle you'll get a sweet wine that Bo says might go well with a dessert. "It's a different wine than most people are used to tasting. For me it's a little too sweet for a meal. It's more of a social drink, like talking to friends or watching TV."

Right now Courson is comfortable with his simple surroundings, but for this man who thinks of his craft as an art form, he does have aspirations to find a bigger canvas. "I hope to grow into a decent winery one day, but when I started this thing I thought to myself well I'd rather be happy than rich. Looks like I'm going to be happy."

Maybe that's the sweetest reward of a vineyard.

....

Logistics

Directions: Courson's winery is on Highway 22 just outside of Sparta, Georgia. Driving from Milledgeville, start looking for the signs just when you cross over the Hancock County line.

Extra's: Bo also sells wine making things and he'll be happy to tell you a few tricks of the trade if you want to make some at home! As a matter of fact check out the wine recipe on the following page!

Website: www.Coursonswinery.com

Phone: (866) 830-0619

Courson's Winery II

This is Ray's newest venture in downtown Milledgeville, a wine tasting room. He calls it 'the place with class!'

Phone: (478) 414-1499

Hours: Mon.–Sat., 10 a.m.-6 p.m.

Courson's Winery Blackberry Wine Recipe

This recipe makes one gallon of blackberry wine with an alcohol content of 10 percent. To make more than one gallon multiply ingredients by the number of desired gallons. *Always follow labeling instructions on all additives.*

• 4 pounds of blackberries

• 5 pints of water

• Approximately 10 ounces of sugar (adjust sugar to 19 Brix of 25 ounce/gallon) based on 2002 Blackberry crop at Courson's Winery. *Use hydrometer to adjust properly.*

• Peptic enzyme—*follow labeling instructions for amount.*

• One Campden tablet

• One pack of wine yeast

• One teaspoon of yeast nutrient

PROCESS OF PRODUCTION

1. Crush blackberries using a potato masher. Put in primary fermentor.

2. Add the five pints of water.

3. Put one teaspoon of yeast nutrient in primary fermentor.

4. One Camden tablet (potassium meta bisulfate). Put in

primary fermentor. Crush the tablet.

5. Adjust temp to 70 degrees F.

6. Let stand for 24 hours.

7. Using hydrometer test the sugar content. Adjust sugar to 25 ounces per gallon or 19 brix. At the the winery the 2002 crop needed 10 ounces dry sugar—9, if you want higher alcohol content. Add more sugar using the potential alcohol scale on your hydrometer.

8. Add wine yeast. One package will do for up to five gallons.

9. Twice daily, press cap (pulp will float to the surface) into wine. This is to extract color.

10. Sugar content reaches 3 Brix or 4 ounces of sugar per gallon. Rack and press. (3-5 days) Put in airtight carboy with air lock to allow the carbon dioxide to escape.

11. When sugar content reaches 0 Brix rack (3 weeks), from here on never pour your wine always siphon or use a wine pump. If your wine does not reach 0 sugar, call for advice.

12. Rack as often as necessary to clear wine.

13. Filter (not necessary if you let wine stand long enough.)

14. Add 1/2 teaspoon of potassium sorbate to stabilize wine. (Refer to labeling instructions.)

15. Sweeten by adding sugar to taste (like sweetening ice tea).

16. Bottle.

FLOWERS
FOR SALE
SEE RAY
1 block over!
452-2036
for info.

DAYLILY
SALE

*Ray's form
of advertising*

Ray tending to his flowers

Ray's Daylilies

I t's amazing how sometimes our lives run parallel to our parents. You might say that's the case with Ray Hemphill. His mom loved daylilies. She loved them so much she had a very young Ray out there weeding as a kid, and then hitting the dirt again many years later when he retired from Robins Air Force Base. Ray's mom died in the early 1980s and he did the only thing left to do. "Well she thought so much of the flowers, I dug up all the lilies and bulbs I could, then some of her friends gave me bulbs too." Ray is quite a gardener himself but he knew he needed more space for the 100 new plants he brought in, so he bought a vacant lot and began making it beautiful. "The flowers I had back then didn't cover the lot so I just started buying flowers and that was ten or eleven years ago."

Now the former, as he calls it, pencil pusher became a petal pusher! He sells six to seven hundred varieties and although he can't remember the official names for all of them he has his favorites. "I like the Chicago Apache. It's a dark red and originally my wife bought it in the 70s from Albany, Georgia." The Apache shares space with Shady Lady, Golden Prize and Black Plush. Ray says the former blooms out like a spider. The thousands of shoots reside in a hideaway that sits only a few yards from the busy highway 49. It's a refuge that's close enough to advertise (you can't help to look from the road) yet dense enough to make you feel like you've found a roadside garden to rest in. Ray loves to visit and keeps a couple of old timey green metal garden chairs ready and waiting for company. "Some people just love to sit there and talk. I don't rush them unless a clouds coming up!"

Rain isn't good for business but it is good for the flowers, although Ray says even a person with the brownest thumb could succeed in growing these colorful stalks. "If you plant one this year, you'll have two next year. Keeping the weeds out is the only thing you have to do. Just plant them, forget them, and watch them grow."

The prices run anywhere from some change to a few dollars for a plant. But expect to find some extra greenery in your bag. "I usually go, if you buy fifteen dollars I'll give you some free ones. The more you buy the more stuff I throw in!"

Ray plans to always have his hands in the dirt, for this son of a gardener this whole experience has sprouted into a way of life. "I enjoy the people as much as anything and anytime you plant a seed and it comes up as a two foot daylily it's satisfying. I have my chair over there—I'll sit back and relax—have an adult beverage and enjoy the blooms and the butterflies."

....

Logistics

Phone: (478) 452-2036

Directions: From Macon take highway 49 to the outskirts of Milledgeville (about 25-27 miles). Look for Ray's big white sign on the side of the road. If Ray's not in the field you can find him at home in his woodshop on Hickory Drive which is one block over! By the way he has a lot of woodwork for sale too!

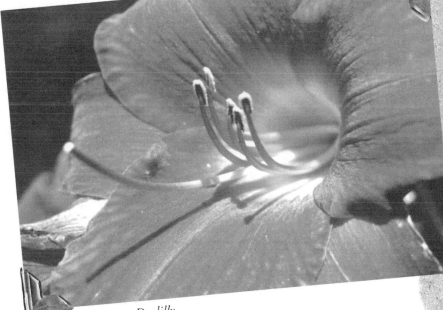

Blooming Daylilly

Truett hanging with a friend

Easy directions to help out on the Maize

The Rock Ranch

This tale begins with a bit of irony. You see Truett Cathy is the guy who started the giant fast food restaurant Chick-Fil-A. They sell chicken—lots of it—and have a very successful advertising campaign with cows toting the benefits of the bird, trying to save their own burger hides. But Cathy farms cattle. And one of his working cattle farms is on The Rock Ranch.

"I was in Truett's Sunday school class when I was 13." Jeff Manley's known and worked with the Cathy family for years. He played a hand in turning the 750-acre cattle land into a custom made country adventure. "Well we made the mistake of letting one Sunday school class picnic out by the pond. Now we have 30-40 thousand people come by a year," he said jokingly.

They come for a variety of reasons. You can visit the petting zoo, fish in the ponds, dress up the goats, take your picture with the cows, get on board for the train ride, play cow patty Bingo (use your imagination you're probably right on the mark) or stay in the cottage they've named the "Bed No Breakfast!" For folks who like to camp out under the stars, giant and I do mean giant, covered wagons sit out in a field complete with eight bunk beds inside and all the crickets and cows joining together for an overnight symphony. All of the above is certainly entertaining, but during the fall season the real draw is the corn maize!

The maize spreads out over 16 acres. Every year you wind your way through a different themed puzzle. One year they had a "Eat more chicken" theme, and then in 2003 they went with the Crayola motif. Mapping out the designs is tough enough but Jeff says actually growing the stuff at the right time is challenging too. "It's a lot of work because you're really fighting Mother Nature. You want it to be green later than it wants to be green so we plant it two months late." But before the tractors do the planting Jeff's gotta map it all out on paper. "Well on this Crayola one I drew in my family as stick figures, so I say if you can get through Abigail and Abel you can get home!" Getting through and getting home is of course the goal as you stomp through a trail laden with flattened corn husks with tall plants lining the path. But don't worry, you do get lots of help. It all works on a passport system. When you walk up you can choose a variety of cards to take you through. By answering the questions right you get prompts to turn right or left. Even if you don't get the answers right corn cops dot the landscape sitting in deer stands to yell down some clues! And Jeff says no one has had to spend the night lost in the field.

But night time is another opportunity for fun. "Well when it gets dark you can go through the maize again with glow sticks or flash lights. "That is so much fun," said Jeff.

At night is also when the bonfire gets crackling and the folks serve up the roasted corn as a snack.

Just one last thing that puts this place close to my heart, this is a setting where adults can play right alongside the kids. It doesn't matter how big or small you are, just climb into the corn box. It's a take off on a sandbox complete with 5880 pounds of kernels! "Adults can do everything, they can get on the tricycles for all we care." And don't forget about the roller slide and the pumpkin decorating art class and the corn cannon!

It's a lot to do over a day but that's okay, you can always come back. "We want to make money but we say we offer an experience in agratainment, we really enjoy smiling faces."

··

Logistics

Phone: (706) 647-6374
Website: www.therockranch.com
Address: The Rock Ranch is located at 5020 Barnesville highway. It's between Lamar and Upson county in The Rock, Georgia on Highway 36.
Admission Prices: Eight dollars per person get you into the Rock ranch to do everything. You can also find coupons at some Chick Fil-A restaurants in the area. Kids five and under get in free!
Seasonal Events: The corn maize and bonfire celebrations go on nightly in the fall. Right around the Fourth of July the Rock Ranch does have a giant fireworks display called Celebrate America. You can camp, or have weekends, or company retreats anytime of the year.

The Falls

High Falls State Park

I've got to admit whenever I want to get away from things I throw my fishing pole in the truck and take off for High Falls. Even though this area isn't known for its rugged outdoor trails like North Georgia, we do have one of the most scenic and peaceful waterfalls in the area. But because of location a lot of folks pass it by without ever appreciating what they're seeing.

"Most everybody says, is that the waterfall, and I say no, that's the dam." Ranger Daniel Ferrone loves working at the place. He says it's a different kind of a landscape than you'll see in other places in Central Georgia. "It's real pretty. It's like the jewel in Middle Georgia because everything else is so flat. There aren't many places you can go close your eyes and hear the water. I've even just laid out on the rocks to hear the birds chirping."

So to make your way to the waterfall after you pass by and see the dam, park you car, walk across the street, and from there you'll take a trail that's not too difficult to walk down. It's mostly full of stone lined steps. You'll start to hear the roar of the water as it quickens its pace alongside where you're walking. And then as you descend you'll see the show play out on your right. At the base the water shoots down 236 yards down the waterfall. It's breathtaking, but maybe I'm a little biased. I love the place. But even if you don't dig waterfalls, there's a lot more to grab your attention. Ferrone says High Falls ranks fourth in the state attendance and maybe that has something to do with the anglers cruising around on High Falls Lake. "We've got 650 acres and 22 miles of shoreline," said Ferrone, "an EPD guy came out here and said this was the best lake in the state to fish that nobody knew about…they're out there man, big ones!"

The park also has ample space for campers who want to spend some time along the river. Terry Regennipter invited me to sit in the air conditioning which in camper's terms means park yourself in front of the fan. Terry and his friend Linda Cahill travel around in their big brown and grey motor home. When they first saw High Falls they knew they'd be back. "I love the waterfall," said Linda. But Terry likes the land. "The most important thing to me is they've left all of the old trees and timber so you have the shade and the coolness. When you have all of that you have the birds and the animals."

The animals, the water, and the tranquility all call High Falls home. Stop by for an hour or for the night, just make sure you don't mistake the dam for the real attraction down the trail!

....

Logistics

Website: You can find out information on all of Georgia's state parks by logging onto www.gastateparks.org.
Phone: (478) 993-3053
Directions: Coming from Macon take I-75 north towards Atlanta. The park is just past Forsyth in Jackson, Georgia. Hang a right off Exit 198 and you'll see the dam and the entrance to the park a couple miles up the road on your right.
Land: High Falls State park has 112 campsites available.

CHAPTER 2

Restaurants

The south is known for its food.
Just imagine fried chicken,
steaming biscuits, and bubbling
peach cobbler. In Central Georgia
the hospitality comes easy and
the plates come piled high with
the goodness from the area.

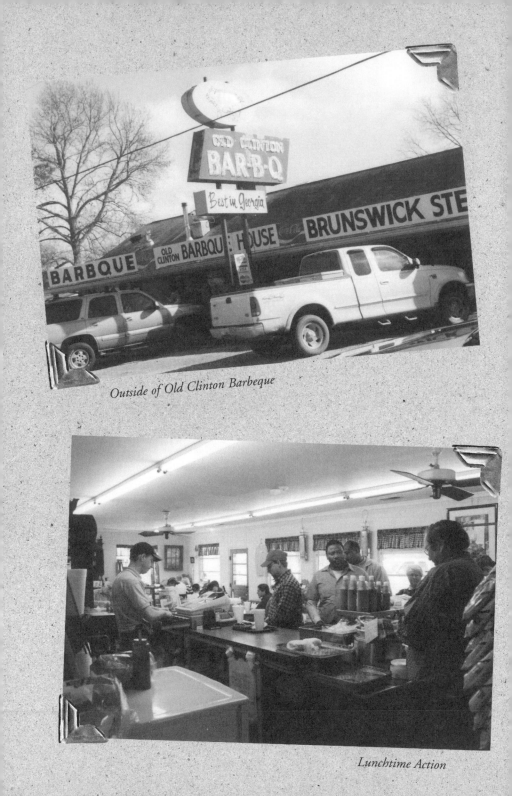

Outside of Old Clinton Barbeque

Lunchtime Action

Old Clinton Barbeque

F olks in Central Georgia can thank the department of transportation for one of the best-known barbeque places in Jones County.

"We used to be in the motel business and then the highway came along." Wayne Coulter was just a kid when all of that happened. Now decades later he's still running the business that sprung up out of a family hobby. "Used to cook all of the time round here, you know Christmas, the Fourth of July." Wayne's dad took his son to another pork place in town before they opened Old Clinton and made good on their grilling. "Yea we visited Fresh Air Barbeque and got some ideas." His Dad started the place up but his Mom made it famous. The elder Mr. Coulter died in 1962, but Mrs. Coulter who everyone called "Lady" stayed in the kitchen pulling pork all the way into her eighties.

But as Wayne will tell you, the meat is just a conduit to the sauce. This one's of course a family recipe with vinegar laying claim to the main ingredient. "People ask for the recipe every day, I tell them good luck," Wayne said with a grin.

Steve Albanese is a fella who grins every time he sits down to the table at Old Clinton. Albanese is a self proclaimed barbeque lover. He's tasted tidbits from all over the southeast. But when he came to Georgia to interview for a pastoral job at the local Baptist church, the committee knew how to tempt their guy. "Well the committee brought me here, they wanted me to know that they had good local barbeque, it was a way to lure me into the area."

The man of God also says he likes the simple surroundings and granted Wayne and his family never went for too many modern upgrades. As you walk in sawdust sits on the welcome mat and inside its plain brown tables and gray concrete floors. Pictures of the matriarch and patriarch hang on the wall while porcelain pigs dot the landscape. "I can remember we never had a menu board for the first thirty years. All we had then was stew and barbeque," said Wayne.

Even if that menu still stood today (turkey and chicken now come on the platters) Ray Fitting would stand as a happy camper. "I had my retirement party here. It's the best barbeque on the planet," he said matter-of-factly. You must know folks in the South take their barbeque seriously. Fitting retired as an Air Force Crash Rescue Firefighter so he faced danger on the job, but maybe the only thing doctors worried about was his Old Clinton habit. "I set the squadron high

cholesterol level. It's in the strong three's," he said proudly.
He accomplished that with at least a couple of slabs
of ribs a week.

Now Wayne doesn't want you to sacrifice your health by
making a visit, but he does watch the health of his business.
He's got the next generation, his stepchildren, in training to
take over one day. And as he fills orders and goes about the
day to day routine he knows his Mom is looking down but
things have changed. "I don't know if she could keep up
now," says Wayne. Maybe not with hundreds of pounds
going out the door every week, but it doesn't matter because
Lady laid the groundwork.

Logistics

Directions: Two miles south of Gray on Highway 129.
Phone: (478) 986-3225
Hours: Open 7 days a week.

You can buy the sauce by itself. The family started bot-
tling it about four years ago.

Dog ready to go

Grillside View

Nu-Way

Folks may know Macon for a few special things that stand out among others—the Cherry Blossom Festival (See p. 155), Southern Hospitality, and Nu-Way Weiners!

A guy by the name of James Mallis thought he had something with his hotdog so he opened the first Nu-Way back in 1916 on Cotton Avenue. Now they have nineteen places that serve up the famous red hotdog, but my favorite is still the original. That's where I met Veronica Guyton. This spunky manager told me Nu-Way is in her blood. "My Mom, my Grandmother, and my Aunt used to work here," she said. Now she's following the family tradition, working behind the grill building burgers and friendships. "Most people that come in here are regulars, we know what they want, don't ask me how we remember them all, we just know," she said. That's quite a feat because Nu-Way is world famous. The place has gotten numerous write-ups locally and garnered national attention. The bright hotdog showed up on PBS, CNN, and Money Magazine.

Okay, so let's break down the tasty treat: An "All the Way" will run you a buck thirty-four. Back in the olden days you could get one for seventeen cents but those days are long gone. "Some kids say, oh it's red. One little boy thought I put ketchup on it, but I didn't. It's just red," explained Guyton. The color is thanks to a red dye. But moving right along, the waitresses slide on the chili, onions, mustard and a dab of barbeque sauce. If you want a twist on the meal get a slaw dog that comes with, of course, slaw, mustard, and ketchup. Okay, now to complete this lesson you've gotta get down the language because if you walk into any NuWay around lunchtime folks sling around the terms like they sling around the chili. It's simple. If you want everything mentioned above just say I want a hotdog or a "dog!" Veronica says "one of each" means a hotdog and a hamburger. And a "one and one" means a hotdog, a hamburger, and a fry!

Veronica explains people will say they come for the chili, but she thinks it has more to do with the atmosphere. "I believe people feel at home in all of them." The decor will take you back a few years. At the shop on Cotton Avenue you can sit at the counter just inches away from all of the action or hang out in the back booths. Lining the wall you'll find advertisements and restaurant gadgets that have played a part through the decades. Veronica says word's got around,

"We've got the regulars but we've had people from Japan and one guy from Russia gave me his business card." Kind of makes the advertising slogan ring true, (insert music and deep voice) "I'd go a long way for NuWay!

....

Logistics

Nu-Way has seven locations in Macon, three in Warner Robins and one in Fort Valley.

Phone (Cotton Avenue): (478) 743-6593

Website: www.nu-wayweiners.com

Incidentals: Be sure you get something to drink with your order, they have great crushed ice. Plus, Nu-Way serves breakfast.

The Sweet Potato Queens

Bowls of food getting ready to go

Buckner's

I f you go to Buckner's restaurant in Jackson, Georgia, get
ready for a big serving of food, gospel singing, and
southern hospitality.

It's the kind of place where folks sit down at huge tables
garnered by a lazy Susan that spins around with mounds of
chow. According to the day of the week, you know what's on
the menu but you never know who will sit down beside you.
But I'm getting a little ahead of myself. Let's start from the
beginning.

Buckner's is a family restaurant. The Buckner's started
with a barbeque place called Homefolks Corner. That
worked out okay but after a little while in business the
family sold the shop. David Buckner thought to himself,
why not try a nine-to-fiver, so he latched on with Delta air-
lines. "For 18 months he hated it, punching the clock," said
his wife Cindy. So the Buckner's went back to what they
knew and what they enjoyed, but even that didn't come easy.

Cindy says where the restaurant sits now (you can see it from I-75) used to be a clothing store. "Well we had to re-do everything to make it a restaurant. It took about a year to open. People thought we were crazy to open that kind of a restaurant around here. There was nothing like there is now, no truck stops or anything!" It took five years for Buckner's to start building a reputation. "We didn't advertise on billboards, you can't when you're not making any money. We just went with word of mouth," she said. But that word of mouth paid off and now 23 years later folks regularly lineup out the door for a hearty helping of home cooked food.

The fried chicken stands as the star. It comes out on every tray, with a supporting cast on various days of barbeque pork, roast beef, cream styled corn, lima beans, coleslaw, Brunswick stew, and a finishing touch of peach cobbler.

But hey a lot of places serve great food, but not a lot of places let you mingle at dinner with the luck of the draw of folks passing by. Case in point, when I stopped by I noticed a group of women having a good time at a table, so I sat down. That's where I met the Sweet Potato Queens Pam Dedeaux, June Papendick, and Debbie Cooper believe in the simple things in life. Their philosophy says it all. "Sweet Potato Queens would like to wear a tiara on their head everyday," Pam explained with a grin. Well who doesn't want a little royalty in their life, but these ladies take that a step farther. Debbie told me Pam had boots and batons on the mantel and that she would mow the lawn in a boa and a tiara if she could. Since I could see that I sat down in the company of women who enjoyed the finer things in life, I asked them why they liked the simple surroundings of Buckner's. "Sweet Potato Queens like to eat in places like this. They were raised on it. It's what your mamma cooked. You just have to pig out," she explained. Debbie, not to be outdone by her friend, chipped in, "It's like going to somebody's house who's a really good cook." The Sweet Potato Queens do have their own unusual reputation of sorts, but Cindy says you just never know who you'll rub elbows with at a meal. "Randy Travis (huge country singer) came in and no-one knew who he was. He just acted like normal but the people he sat down with just went crazy," she said.

Randy could have joined other folks on the Buckner's stage. Every Thursday, Friday and Saturday nights they put on free gospel and bluegrass concerts. It's something this religious family did to give back to the person they blame their success on. "Our biggest thing is we thank God for it." So between the food, the people, and the music check out Buckner's for a complete, and I do mean complete, dining experience!

Logistics

Directions: From Macon head up I-75 north towards Jackson, Georgia. Turn and head to the left off of exit 201.
Hours: Closed Monday and Tuesday. Wednesday they're open from 11-3. Thursday, Friday, and Saturday they're open for lunch and dinner.
Phone: (770) 775-6150 (Groups of 20 or more can call ahead. Cindy says that helps out!)

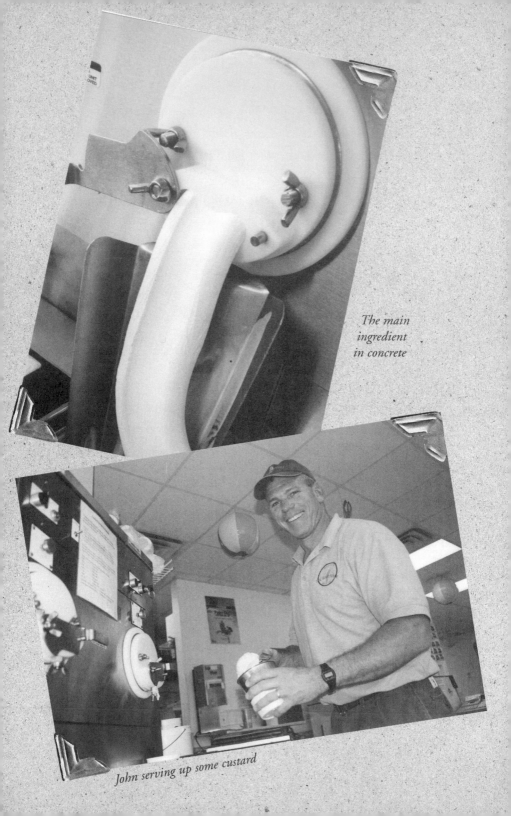

The main
ingredient
in concrete

John serving up some custard

The Boardwalk

"**I**'ll skip meals so I can eat ice cream." With words like that you've got to think John Teague is in the right business.

He runs a frozen custard shop in Warner Robins called The Boardwalk. Even though this guy knows dairy (he spent time on a dairy farm as a teenager) he admits when it comes to inspiration for everything else in the shop he doesn't mind copying. "I'm not creative at all. If it were up to me we would have black walls and vanilla custard." The place is far from that. He has 71 flavors on the menu—creations like chocolate malted almond, cherry pie with cheesecake pie crust, and caramel cashew. Teague says if you can dream it he'll try and create it. "But I do make them eat it to see if they'll survive," he chuckled. There's another tool in the resourcefulness sack. "There's thirty custard places in Milwaukee and I've been to all of them picking up menus," he explained. "My parents will pick up sandwich menus from all over the place." Even one of his main sellers, the concrete (which is a thick frozen custard with a bunch of good stuff swirled inside), comes from a guy he calls the Dali Lama of frozen custard. "Ted Drew is well known with his place out on route 66. It's like the Varsity in Atlanta. Anyway, he started concretes that you can get by the half a yard or the yard," he said. "Little kids get the terminology but the adults can't figure out if that's one scoop or two!"

It is hard to describe custard in a scoop. Custard ice cream got started along the Boardwalk on Coney Island in the early 1900s but there is still plenty of confusion to what's in it. "If you say frozen custard people think oh eggy pie." It's not pie. It is an ice cream, but by law it's gotta have 1.4 percent egg yolks in the mix. The Boardwalk's mix also contains ten percent butterfat (commercial ice creams normally range from 12-14 percent butterfat). Teague says a good mix is the most important ingredient. Special machines take over fluffing air into the recipe and finally Teague says a frozen custard is best served within a few hours of being made.

While sitting in a booth I did hear a complaint from a very young customer. I overheard him grumble because the fresh peach custard had too many chunks of peaches. Teague just laughed and said "next time we'll take a few out for him."

Logistics

Address: 1241 Russell Parkway, Warner Robins, Georgia
Phone: (478) 922-2111

Custard reigns supreme but you can also order sandwiches, shaved ice, and espresso.

Phillip and Betty.

Miss Louise conjuring up her next great recipe

Forsyth Square Restaurant and Inn

"It really did come out of left field." That's how Phillip Mock describes his current position as an innkeeper and owner at the Forsythe Square Restaurant and Inn. Phillip's wife Betty went along with him on a baseball tournament trip to Savannah. As the couple made their way home to Alpharetta, Georgia, Betty whipped out the newspaper. She said "I want to stop here (at the time it was called the Farmhouse and it was for sale)." Phillips obligingly said "Yes, Dear," with a grin. You've got to understand this couple is the epitome of Laurel and Hardy. Phillip (the contemplative one) had a career in hospital administration. Betty is the vivacious talker. She was working as an interior designer before they bought the bed and breakfast in Forsythe. The duo said they had no hesitations about dropping their careers, packing up their stuff, and moving to a town that is quite on the other end of the spectrum from Alpharetta.

"We wanted to get back that sense of community. We didn't have any connections and Alpharetta had gotten too big," said Betty.

So now the two walk around in casual clothes and chat with the customers although Phillip says he can't get a word in edgewise. Most stop by for a meal. It's a meat and two vegetable kind of place. A dining room where the waitresses sit down and chat with you at the table. The buffet line is full of southern cuisine. "You gotta have fried chicken," said Betty. They have the old standbys and whatever Miss Louise puts her personal touch on. "She's been here fifteen years, never called in sick, and she's never late." said Betty.

As for the Inn part, the Mock's have 11 rooms, all pretty much decorated with antiques and southern charm, with one exception. "There is a pepto-bismol room," said Phillip. That one's a little more feminine with pinks and baby dolls. If you stop by be sure to ask them about the coach that had to take a good deal of ribbing from his team for a night of slumber in that one.

And although the couple has settled in for a few years to their new life, Phillip is still amazed by the questions folks ask. "About ten thirty at night the phone rings," he starts explaining, "this woman was calling on her cell asking about the rooms and she asks me, 'Are they clean?' I immediately asked her are you clean?" Betty chimes in, "I can't believe you said that!" "Anyway, the couple did come to stay but when they walked through the door they said, do you have any restrooms!"

Phillip still laughs about that one and for the record they do have clean rooms and restrooms with all of the accommodations.

The Mocks say they'll stay put for awhile. Betty even thinks one day she'll take a run at the Mayor's office. But maybe the most telling sign that these two have found a place to call home is the simple fact that Betty doesn't look at the newspaper anymore!

....

Logistics

Phone: (478) 994-2165

Directions: Downtown Forsyth across from the backend of the courthouse.

If you spend the night, room rates which start at forty-nine dollars a night include breakfast.

Diane behind the grill

Chili Dog

English's Café

Before the Roseanne show on TV, I never knew about loose meat sandwiches, but there is a place in Thomaston, Georgia where the meat is as loose as the wagging tongues that make up the conversation around the bar. The place actually has its roots in the saloon business. It dates back to the late 1920s, but in the 1950s the English Café doubled as the town's pool hall. "If you were any kind of a respectable woman you didn't go in the pool room. Only people with loose morals would come in," said Diane Jones. Times have changed and now Diane is the woman behind the counter serving up sandwiches all day long. She's the kind of person who may never remember your name, instead calling you sugar, baby, or honey, but she'll nail down the important stuff. "I don't know people by their name, I know them by what they eat," she explained.

It's not a lot to memorize in the way of food. The menu mainly consists of hamburgers that come with chili, mustard, and onion and hotdogs that sit plump in a dish and hold on to a generous portion of chili, oyster crackers, onions, and mustard. (You have to ask for ketchup.) One hotdog is definitely a meal, but for health conscious folks they do make up a tasty chicken salad. On the other hand if you want the saucy meat, "I tell folks I take all the fat and calories out," said Diane. In a world with restaurants branching out their menus daily, there is a simple reason why you only get a few choices at the English Café. "People like things simplified. You change things on people in this town they nut up," explained Diane.

By the looks of the place things haven't changed in decades. Yellow walls hang onto relics of the past like milk jugs, Coca-cola signs and railroad crossing ties. You will even see an ancient coffee grinder. "This is identical to the one on Little House on the Prairie," explained Diane. The main part of the small restaurant sits up front, a big four sided square counter with the original cast iron stove sitting smack in the middle. Gas burners cook up the meat and help to add the slightly greasy, spicy smell to the place. The red weathered Formica has slight indentations where folks have rested quite a many elbows eating quite a many meals. You may notice one of the stools sits about eight inches higher than the rest. There's a story. "It was because of Shorty, he was short and when he sat on a regular stool he couldn't reach the counter, so they raised that one, and when customers would come in they would give up the stool so he could have his seat." Shorty's gone but the reputation of the loose meat burger lives on. "Anyone born in Upson County has eaten a hamburger here," said Marvin Ingram as he perched up on a stool. "The ones that have left, this is the first thing you do when you come back is get a couple of burgers and it's the first thing you do before you leave town again. I don't know about the rest of the state but this is the burger to eat."

On average Diane will put 30 pounds of ground chuck into the frying pan a day and then work through crumbling it up with a tool that breaks it all apart. But of course the key is the chili and I did ask for the recipe. "I can't tell you that, except that I cook it on top of the stove. I put this and that in and I cook it," said Diane.

You may not get the ingredients but the whole place is a recipe for a tasty meal with good conversation on the side.

Logistics

Location: It's right on the square in downtown Thomaston
Phone: (706) 647-5525
Hours: 11:00 AM-7:00 PM Monday through Friday, Saturday 11:00 AM –5:00 PM. Closed on Sundays.
Incidental: Paschal English (guy who made it to the final four on the CBS show Survivor and lives in Thomaston) isn't at all related to the Café.

Shrimp and Grits

Wayne stirring up a pot of grits

Grits Café

There is probably nothing more southern food wise, than the humble little grit. For you Yankees, grits by definition consist of small broken grains of corn. Now that may not sound like the tastiest treat in the land, but here in our neck of the woods we pile butter, sugar, and cheese to make a meal. One man decided to take things a bit farther.

"There is so much you can do with them. The possibilities are endless," says Wayne Wetendorf explaining the namesake of his restaurant, the Grits Café.

Wayne's cooked, or in this guy's case we should say created, dishes all over the United States. Eventually he and his wife Terri relocated to Forsyth because of her job. Wayne wanted his own place so he hit the internet looking for a niche. "There was nothing upscale in this area. I couldn't believe it."

Ironic that he paired upscale with grits, but then again you've never seen the way Wayne whips up ground up corn. The menu changes but an old standby is shrimp and grits. At anytime you might find a Grits gourmet burger, a sweet Vidalia onion tart with a savory Grits crust, grits fritters, or a salad with asiago grits croutons.

Now don't get the wrong idea, you won't find grits in your drinks, or hidden in your dessert. "We don't want to overdo it," said Wayne. That's why the grits only accent a menu heavy with fresh seafood entries and smattered with dishes like pecan crusted pork medallions or chicken breasts stuffed with asparagus and served with a lobster chardonnay sauce. As a matter of fact he describes the Grits Café experience as "Nouveau Southern."

Well I'm not sure what Nouveau Southern is (too many trips to the Nu-Way I guess) but I can tell you when you walk in you immediately feel at home. The place is lightly sponge painted in a peach color accented by lavender shutters and borders. Tiny white lights sit in wrapped vines of Kudzu. Patches of exposed brick highlight the walls (Wayne says the building used to stand as the Forsyth Mercantile) and share the space with colorful oil paintings done by a local artist. Three antique gas lamps light up at night. Jazz music permeates throughout the place that at any one time can seat 96 grits lovers! "People come in and see it, then they experience the service and taste the food and they say Wow," explained Wayne, "they just don't expect this kind of thing in a small town."

Dawn Hagan and Ginny Sapp live in the area and admit they sit down to a table about twice a week. "At least, and if it's anyone's birthday we're here," said Dawn. "You can come in here all dressed up and feel fancy yet we've been in here in jeans and shorts." As Ginny told me to save room for dessert Dawn went on about the menu. "We like home cooking, you see fancy stuff and you think oh, this is going to taste weird, but it doesn't. This does taste like home cooking," she said.

In honor of Ginny, do try a dessert. This is also a menu that changes periodically. In the summer you can get peaches and cream. In the winter you might get pears served warm in a crème sauce. For the chocolate lovers Wayne makes a turtle sundae made with Milky Way ice cream in a pecan shortbread crust and served with chocolate sauce.

Don't expect anything to come out of the kitchen without some flair, whether it's a little cutout edible cactus on your quesadillas or the piece of pecan lace nut brittle that garnishes every dessert. "I guess the one word to describe me is anal," said Wayne.

And because of that the south may never think of grits again in the same way!

Logistics

Location: The Grits Café is on the square in downtown Forsyth at 17 West Johnston Street.

Phone: (478) 994-8325

Hours: Lunch—Tuesday-Saturday 11-2. Dinner: Tuesday, Wednesday and Thursday, 5:30-9, Friday and Saturday, 5:30-10.

Reservations: Only for parties of six or more.

Incidentals: Everyday on the lunch and dinner menu Wayne has something called a runaway and a blue-plate. Those are recipes that change everyday.

Hot Fudge Sundae!

Relax on the sprawling front porch

The Scoope Shop

D onna Asbell grew up in Irwinton, Georgia. She moved away, but when the family house sat empty for ten years and her parents thought about selling the place, Donna came home. In some ways she re-created her childhood and set out to make this little town a little bit sweeter.

Now the little house where Asbell's dad would pick the first bi-color camellia of the season for her mom, Donna picks and chooses the types of ice cream and antiques you might want to savor for your family.

Let's take a tour! In the Scoope Shoppe you might hunker down for a Blast from the Past Sundae. They start with an old fashioned Moon Pie, topped with your favorite ice cream (they have eight flavors to choose from), laced with chocolate syrup, sprinkled with crunchy peanuts, and finished off with a cherry on top! Donna helped create this concoction for one simple reason. "Some kids have never had Moon Pies."

Well if retro food is your thing, head on over to the candy room. It used to serve as Donna's brothers abode but now the black, white, and red motif serves as a back drop for just about every candy you can imagine including the ones that ruled kids taste buds decades ago. Sugar Daddy's, Penny Candy, Fire Shocks, Tootsie Rolls, and Grandma's cookies sit piled high in jars.

Adults can wander through the florist and antique area. You'll find all kinds of stuff. After your shopping feel free to relax in the back courtyard. Adirondack chairs sit perched next to a bubbling rock fountain. The front porch offers a nice respite too with rocking chairs and green vines claiming their space running up the supports with a peaceful view of the town.

It's a different kind of place with one simple central theme running throughout. "When I was a kid there was a store in Irwinton that had penny candy," Donna explained. "We'd always go down there, we wanted a place like that and I think we've done it. Little kids walk or ride their bikes here."

Big kids have a chance to get in on the fun too. Thursday is game night in the candy room. But Donna has a bigger vision to bring everyone in Irwinton together. "I'd like to do a Saturday tennis tournament (a court neighbors the shop) with croquet games in the field with maybe a senior tea party. We just want it to be more than a place to come and shop."

Asbell's says her parents are proud of what their daughter's created on the land where they raised the family. Although the transition did come with some bumps. "It did take some adjustment taking down the walls, and it's hard to cut down a tree your Mom planted."

But now Asbell's planting the seeds for a place in town where people can enjoy a bowl of ice cream and conversation on the porch. Maybe that's really the sweetest treat of all.

Logistics

Phone: (478) 946-2818

Address: 128 East Main Street, Irwinton, Georgia. When you drive into town on Highway 57 in the middle of town the road forks, bear to the left. The Scoope shop is two scoops down the road on your right.

Website: www.extrahoursonline.com

Hours: Monday-Wednesday 9-6 p.m., Thursday and Friday 9-7 p.m., Saturday 10-7 p.m.

Extra's: Donna does all kinds of parties including a midnight bash for teenagers that want to come and have snacks in their pajamas. Plus, if you love milkshakes, order one up. The Scoope Shoppe recipe comes with a bit of Karo Syrup in every glass. It makes quite a difference!

Homemade cakes sit on the counter

Gena and her sister Lynn running the family business

Maebob's

The people at Maebob's restaurant tell folks they are located right in the heart of Irwinton, Georgia. That's definitely accurate but it might be easier to say they're the only restaurant in Irwinton, Georgia!

Maebob's opened back in 1976. Two women in the Bicentennial of America decided to blend each other's nicknames May and Bob and go into business. The original entrepreneurs retired and now 27 years later the next generation of daughters call the shots from behind the counter. "We never figured it would last this long." Gena Blizzard started working at Maebob's as a teenager. She never left. She thinks the place is successful for two reasons. "Well it is the only place, but I think we do have some kind of charm." That they do, as plates piled high with good country cooking stream out of the kitchen, folks sit in bright yellow booths with reminders of Irwinton decking the walls.

In this small town folks can depend on daily favorites to stay on the menu. Homemade cornbread compliments stewed beef on Monday's. On tuesdays chicken and dressing take center stage. Wednesday, pork chops pop out of the oven. Thursday means meatloaf and Friday the fish sit perched on the plates. It never changes and that's okay. "I don't think they get tired of it. They keep coming back." Now don't think everything is as rigorous as the daily special. People can order off a menu that has everything from sandwiches to steaks. Plus customers have been known to come up with their own concoctions. "Well along with the rotisserie chicken, the stewed tomatoes, and the cabbage, I love the French fries with gravy on top. You've got to try it, it's really good." Dinah Harrison eats Maebob's cuisine a couple of times a week. She thinks the restaurant survived because if you want French fries with brown gravy on top—hey, no problem. It's all part of the charm. "It is the only restaurant in town, but it has good food. Other restaurants have tried but they failed."

It would be hard for another place to break the tradition that's developed in this simple, homey atmosphere. "In the morning the same men come in drink coffee and talk," said Gena. "All the gossip is passed here. All the deputies and the sheriff come by. It's just central to everybody," said Dinah.

Dinah also recommends you save room for dessert. A local housewife brings by three homemade cakes a day in the kind of Tupperware containers your Mom would lug along to the family picnic. Some of the flavors include moist strawberry cake with of course bright pink icing, devil's food with peanut butter topping and a few other distinct culinary treats.

In this restaurant where family pictures sit proudly by the cash register and quite a few cooks have spent decades churning out country meals maybe the answer to the proverbial question isn't hard at all. Sure, Maebob's is the only restaurant in Irwinton, but really, who would need anything else?

....

Logistics

Phone: (478) 946-8940

Directions: From Macon take highway 57 about 30 miles right into the heart of downtown Irwinton. You can't miss Maebob's at the one stop light on the town square.

Drop dollars in the tasting jug

Sign outside the tasting room

Habersham Winery

In the movie *Fried Green Tomatoes*, the two main characters Idgy and Ruth never drank a glass of wine, but Betty Clements thinks history could have played out differently on the movie set. "They were drinking beer and whiskey, but I'm sure if they had the Habersham Winery they would have had wine." Maybe she's right because when the movie went into production in Juliette, Betty's place didn't exist yet. She came in later and at first just sold antiques and gifts. But her daughter saw room for expansion. "Denise likes wine and she looked around and said man, that would make a great wine cellar." At the time Betty did have a wonderful downstairs part of her space. It was dark, stony and when you walked downstairs the temperature fell by at least ten degrees. "Well it was used for storage then. It had hay, wood, and it's own snake. We tried to shoot the snake but that didn't work but we did clean it all up and called the Habersham Winery."

The Habersham winery liked the idea. They grow Georgia grapes and put out a splendid array of wines. They only have five tasting rooms in the state. But unfortunately Betty's perfect cellar flooded in August 2003 after a particularly ferocious thunderstorm. And at the time of this writing she's not sure she'll risk going back downstairs with her stock. But all is not lost, Betty re-created everything upstairs and thinks it's going to work out. "It's still the wine and it's still us. I think my son Dean said it best, 'It's not what it was but it is what it is.'"

It's that positive attitude that surrounds Betty's shop. Sure, she sells bottles of wine, but you also get a taste of home just by sitting and talking with her and anyone who stops by. Betty's created a living room, complete with high backed rocking chairs, a heater, and a platform for conversation—any kind of conversation. "We just a gossipin'. You gotta have a place to tell lies at."

And Betty's got some whoppers. I asked her if anyone walked in with a snooty attitude, putting on airs while tasting the wine? "Some really do make a big deal of sipping, but I had one lady ask, where do you spit? I said, ma'am you're in downtown Juliette. I guess you can spit wherever you want!"

Swallowing is probably the best option. Betty will hand you a sheet that looks somewhat like a menu, listing all of the Chardonnays, Rieslings and Merlots. She ranks the

Georgia White Muscadine, the Peach Treat and Granny's Arbor as some of her favorites. But one bottle is close to her heart. It's a 2000 Chambourcin Dessert Wine. "It's very, very rich and it's good. It does help keep all the deer hunters warm!"

Betty asks that you pitch in a buck for a taste but don't get confused, this place isn't a bar. "We just sell by the bottle. It gets carted by little old ladies going back to Ohio."

For this wonderful woman who I must admit is a personal friend things have come full circle. Betty used to play with her best friend over in the big grits mill as a child never dreaming she'd make her livelihood just across the street. So these days as the sun sets you can find Betty and some of the more interesting characters in town sitting around telling stories. The wine sitting in the background is just an excuse to uncork some southern hospitality.

Logistics

Phone: (478) 994-0057

Directions: Follow the directions from the Whistle Stop Café. The Winery is right across the street. Off I-75 at exit 186, go east for nine miles. Juliette is on the right.

Extras: Betty sells many wine-related things and she still has gifts, antiques, and novelties in the shop. As for selling alcohol on Sundays Betty does have a special license that allows her to sell the bottles after 12:30 p.m.

Price's: It's a dollar per taste of wine and the bottles run in price from $12 to $26.

SUZANNE LAWLER

Monique and Karolina

German cuisine laid out on the table

Monique's German Café

If the extent of your culinary experiences with German food only consists of an occasional Bratwurst then you need to make a bee-line for Monique's German Café.

Monique Humphrey just opened her Warner Robins restaurant in May of 2003. But the restaurant business is old hat. The slim, energetic woman with the heavy accent has done this before. "I love it. I used to have a restaurant in Germany." The first place didn't carry her namesake, it was named after a famous German dish called Schwenkbraten, which is a pork sirloin steak marinated for three days. "Everybody asked for it when they came in here so I started to serve it, but I couldn't get the seasoning right so I called a butcher in Germany."

The steak is wonderful, tasty in a way that you can't pinpoint what makes it so delicious. But if you don't want that, you can choose from ten different kind of Schnitzel's off the menu. I see you wondering about the language, so a schnitzel's a breaded piece of pork with various toppings. Monique says the Rahm is the most popular; it comes with mushrooms and cream gravy. But for the more adventuresome there's Holstein, topped with ham cheese and egg, the Zigeuner topped with onions bell peppers and paprika or the Hawaiian sitting under pineapple and Swiss cheese.

And as you may expect in a German restaurant you can also hunker down to a bratwurst or knackwurst. The sauerkraut is made with red cabbage and served warm, while the German potato salad comes cold and is wonderfully delicious with seasonings and vinegar. If you want French fries ask the waitress for pom fritz as opposed to home fries which come out as more of a sliced potato hash brown dish. As for dessert, you can go with the German Cheesecake or the Black Forest cake, but for some real fun order up the Spaghetti ice cream! The staff stuffs the ice cream into a press that resembles something out of a Play-doh shop. It comes out as strings of the sweet treat and then it's topped with strawberry topping and whipped cream. But think about it, all that cranking's hard work. "Now we buy soft ice cream. Before we knew about that we would all say to each other, you do the ice cream, no, you make the ice cream." Even though Karolina Rock complained about building up her muscles with the ice cream, she knew when she walked into Monique's she had to get on the payroll. "I lived in Germany eleven years. I ate here one day and I said 'oh my.' The music made me cry and I said this is my home!" she said reminiscing.

Monique has created a German experience inside the cozy walls. The German music plays all day. It's from her personal collection. Guess it's hard to get German Muzac piped in! Steins and a ton of different German Beers line the walls along with witty sayings. Although the sayings are in German so you'll have to ask for some translation. "Well that one says to the customer who thinks the staff is rude, first meet the boss," Monique laughs. She loves to joke but the saying couldn't be more true. Sure the owner is picky about how things run, she overseas all the cooking and won't give out any of her recipes because she says, "hey why would you come back?" But Monique is quick with a joke and uses mustard packaged like toothpaste as an opportunity to get around and talk to folks eating in the place. "It is special mustard from Germany. When my husband went back I had him get three hundred tubes. You can't get it around here," she said.

"It will light you up!" Master Sergeant Ben Bailey and his wife Sharon like the mustard and love the restaurant. The couple spent three years stationed in Germany so they know what the authentic food should taste like coming out of the kitchen. "We love it, it's where I had my birthday luncheon," Sharon said. "The music really brings back the memories of walking along the streets of Germany. Germans are such festive people," she added. The festive people in Warner Robins want you to walk away happy. And if by chance you order a schnitzel not to your liking, tell the owner. "We don't mind to exchange things because we want to be fair. I love to cook and I want to see the people happy eating the food!"

Logistics

Phone: (478) 929-5251

Hours: 10:30-9:30 p.m. everyday except Sundays, that's when everyone gets a day off.

Directions: Monique's is located at 713 Watson Boulevard. From Macon take Highway 247 into Warner Robins, hang a right on Watson Boulevard and Monique's is only a Schnitzel down the road (very close) across from the Warner Robins Municipal Building.

Larry working with popcorn

Chocolate and peanut butter Buckeyes

McCrackin Street Sweets

You might expect a guy who runs a sweet shop in Juliette, Georgia, to wear an apron that says "Oh Fudge!" But what you may not expect is for the same man to have a background in something quite different.

"Well I got out of the forestry business in the 80s. I just wanted to do something else." So Larry Pierce went into sales and eventually he felt he could make a contribution and a living in candy. He and his family moved their gift and confectionary business to Fried Green Tomatoes town in 1992 but Larry didn't have his hands into making the stuff yet. But he did pride himself on conjuring up some of the "World's Best, Fresh-Squeezed Lemonade." Then a year or two passed and the guy Larry bought his candy from decided to leave the state, but not to worry, he offered to teach Larry the craft of creating candy. As a matter of fact the huge marble table that holds all of the candy coming out of the kettle belonged to the teacher's grandmother!

And now ten years later the man has mastered everything that sits in the case. Everyday he dives into the Divinity, breaks up the brittle, and prepares the pralines. When you walk in the shop you may find him hovering over a big vat of popcorn carefully coating it with caramel or working with mammoth mounds of chocolate patiently turning it all over into a perfect loaf of fudge. Along the way he's even come up with some of his own concoctions. "This is called White Trash. It's got almonds, cashews, peanuts, chocolate chips, and marshmallows all in white chocolate."

Chocolate rules supreme, although on a hot summer day you can also duck in for some freshly squeezed lemonade or a hearty helping of some Hawaiian Ice. The brightly colored bottles of flavor sit upright and ready for their next customer. But hey, enough of that let's get back to the chocolate. If you like the salty-sweet taste go for a real southern treat of Ritz crackers sandwiched with peanut butter and rolled in chocolate. Or peanut lovers pluck up one of my favorites the little buckeyes. Somehow the peanut butter just melts in your mouth under a smidgen of chocolate sitting on top of this little ball. "The Buckeyes are an old recipe but out of all this candy that would be my choice too." Quite an endorsement from a guy who says he gives away a lot of samples but for the most part doesn't touch the stuff he makes everyday. "My biggest downfall is ice cream and that's probably the reason I don't sell it or I would be eating it all the time!"

It's the kind of place you walk in and say, there goes the diet. But it's also the kind of place that Larry has decorated with memories of his past. Light pink walls line the cozy room decked out with antiques and family photos. The décor reminds him of his roots and keeps him hoping that his grandchild may one day follow in Gramps footsteps. "You see right now I'm the only one who can make the fudge. My wife and daughter can make the other candy. Fudge making can get frustrating. Larry says you've got to know when to start creaming the batter and then you just have a minute or so to shape it before it sets! "I hope my grandbaby will be able to pick up the fudge." About all the little guy can do right now is pick it up, but maybe with the right teacher McCrackin Street Sweets will stay in downtown Juliette as a place for you to pick up a decadent little dessert to enjoy after your Fried Green Tomatoes.

Logistics

Hours: Open 7 days a week, Monday-Friday 10-4 p.m. Saturday and Sunday 9-5, or whenever folks stop coming through the doors.
Phone: (478) 994-4498
Website: www.georgiacandy.com
Directions: McCrackin Street Sweets, located in downtown Juliette. Off I-75, take exit 186, go east for nine miles. Juliette is on the right. Look closely for the sign.

Relax on the big Southern front porch

Order of Fried Green Tomatoes

Whistle Stop Café

Someone looking to get into the restaurant business couldn't find a better opportunity than a quaint little café that already comes with a great reputation and a somewhat cult following over the cuisine.

That someone turned out to be Elizabeth Bryant. She was a theft fraud investigator for an insurance company a few years back. Strange, you might say, but not any stranger than how The Whistle Stop café came to life.

"To my knowledge it was originally built in 1927 as a General Merchandise store," Elizabeth explained. Just imagine in a woodsy, smaller-than-small town where folks would come into this place for household, goods, meats, and tools.

Fast forward about seventy years when a movie producer came looking for the perfect set to film the movie *Fried Green Tomatoes*. "It was really only a storage place when the movie people came through." And now it's a living legacy to a movie that made folks laugh and cry. *Fried Green Tomatoes* is pretty much about a housewife (Kathy Bates) who makes friends with a story telling older lady (the late Jessica Tandy) who spins tales surrounding the Whistle Stop café.

Today you can sit in the booths or belly up to the bar that actually appeared as the backdrop for the movie. And even though the film came out years ago, Bryant says folks can't seem to get enough of the Fried Green tomatoes and the atmosphere. "When it's shown on the network we're crowded the next day. People are all over the place saying things like 'oh, I remember that.'"

They remember because not much has changed. A sign out front still totes good food at fair prices. People sit and wait to get in on a big friendly southern wrap-around porch. Inside, the iced tea comes out of the kitchen in Mason jars and the waitresses walk up and greet you by saying, "Can I start you off with some Fried Green Tomatoes?" Tons of movie memorabilia hang on the walls and a very boisterous reminder of the movie comes rumbling down the tracks every couple of hours or so.

"Oh, the train added to the local color and flavor. I was sitting on the porch when it went by." Patrician Peppercorn likes to venture off the beaten path to find new things. Not only did she see the movie but she read the book written by Fannie Flagg. She says she loved the place but it's the food she's going to try and duplicate at home. "These sweet potato fries are very interesting. I've never seen them done with sugar and cinnamon. I'm going to have to try and bake them!"

Basically this is a home-style meat and two veggies place. You can get barbeque or fried chicken. You might ask for the sweet potato soufflé on the side. It comes with big walnuts sticking out and sprinkles of brown sugar on top. But Bryant's added a few new things to the classic menu like the fries and a healthier choice of Fried Green Tomato salad plus a new dessert. "It's an apple dumpling steamed and wrapped in pastry dough and baked with a topping that seems to be a favorite."

But Bryant thinks the Whistle Stop Café continues to be a favorite in part because of Hollywood but also because of a simple southern tradition in town. "People who wouldn't normally receive southern hospitality venture off interstate 75 and they see what southerners are made of. We're good people and around here. It's not a fast pace place."

Just the kind of setting Idgy and Ruth would have approved of long ago.

....

Logistics

Hours: Sunday–Wednesday, 11-4; Thursday–Saturday, 11-7 p.m.; closed on Mondays and open on Tuesdays, 11-4, spring through fall.
Website: www.thewhistlestopcafe.com
Phone: (478) 992-8886
Directions: From Macon go north on Riverside Drive heading out of town. Motor on down the road 14 miles and you will see a small sign on the left hand side of the road. Hang a right on McCrackin Street and wind you way through until Juliette appears just outside your dashboard!

Or, off I-75, take exit 186, go east for nine miles. Juliette is on the right. Look closely for the sign.

CHAPTER 3

Festivals

Central Georgia knows pink.
We turn the lighter shade of red every
March when the city goes all out for
the Cherry Blossom Festival. But the
thing you've gotta realize about the
South is when we're proud of something
we've got to show it off and have a
celebration. That's what you'll find at
all times of the year as the area shows
off its best and sometimes its
questionable every 12 months.

Big Papa Plump and
Lil'Mama Burning Bush

Toilet Seat Toss

Redneck Games

hen I got up in the morning to go to the World Famous Georgia Redneck Games I needed a checklist to get ready.

1) American Flag T-Shirt — check
2) Beer baseball hat — check
3) Shorts with holes — check
4) Deodorant — optional

There's nothing formal about Georgia's southern form of the Olympics. Men with beer bellies and bandanas compete in all kinds of events that your mother never told you about! Everything from dumpster diving to toilet seat horseshoes are on the agenda. Although the one that really draws the crowds in is the Mudpit Belly Flop. Imagine 200 plus guys taking a nosedive into a vat of red Georgia goo. Robert

Kilgore, better known as Big Papa Plump, has the girth to go the distance. "It's real refreshing," he said. But he hasn't won. "Just didn't make a big enough splash," said his wife Lil' Mama Burning Bush. By the way, she got her name when Papa almost set her on fire with his cigarette. While talking game plans and downing another can of beer Papa did give his definition of a redneck. "Somebody that don't truly give a damn what other people think about us," he said. "If you don't like us don't look at us."

It's hard to miss the rednecks this weekend and the one that really stands out (besides Grandma redneck) is Elbow.

This is a character that goes around with six beer cans jimmied together that makes up the official torch for the whole affair. "It lights the ceremonial barbeque," he said.

And as you can see by the photo, he's got that good ol' Georgia redneck face.

If you dare to bare your chest hairs and belch with the best of them here's what you can expect in the way of souvenirs, confederate flags by the crateful, some Georgia moonshine jelly, or the colorful Kudzu flowers (Kudzu is an alien vine that creeps all over everything sent here to destroy the earth). They "hadn't bought didley yet but they will," said Diane Hoots.

Well maybe after the serenade armpit contest!

Logistics

When: The first Saturday after the fourth of July

Directions: From Macon head down Interstate 16 towards Savannah. Take exit 51 and hang a left. Follow the road for a few miles until it curves sharply to the right and you run over some railroad tracks. That will bring you to an intersection. Take a right at the red light onto highway 80. That will take you into East Dublin. Take a left on Buckeye Road heading toward Buckeye Boat Landing. Then just follow the cars in.

Price: $5 for parking

Elbow with a redneck grin

SUZANNE LAWLER

Ralph Hall with a
couple of his whoppers

Friendly Watermelon

Watermelon Festival

I f you've ever heard the country song "Do the "Watermelon Crawl" you've gotta think Tracy Byrd[1] was singing about Cordele Georgia.

I was driving thru Georgia in late July, On a day hot enough to make the Devil sigh, I saw a homemade sign written in red, Rind County Watermelon Festival Ahead; Well, I wasn't in a hurry, so I slowed down, Took a two lane road to a one horse town, There was a party going on when I got there, I heard a welcome speech from a small town mayor.

Every first and second weekend in July Cordele celebrates the mammoth fruit they're known for in the town's Watermelon festival. In the green fields around Crisp County farmers turn out more watermelons than anywhere

---

[1] Tracy Byrd, *No Ordinary Man*, MCA, 1994.

else in the world, so it's no wonder they need a good many days to put the best picks on a pedestal.

Ralph Hall grows some of the heaviest fruit around. His specimens weigh more than many adults and most children. On the back of his truck sits a melon tipping the scales at 184 pounds. Every year he hovers over his plants with a special secret held in a two liter plastic bottle. "I put an IV coke bottle in the dirt," he explains. "Fourteen drops a minute go into the dirt of special solution." He wouldn't discuss his special solution. After all, he's got state records to protect. But suffice it to say, these mammoth melons are pretty much for the eyes only. With all of the chemicals floating around inside the meat, Ralph doesn't let folks dig into his creations.

One little guy who's all about scarfing down some fruit is 12 year-old Taylor Hall. He put his appetite on the line for the watermelon eating contest. In a sticky, soaking wet watermelon drenched t-shirt this little guy shared some strategy for the challenge. "Wear something for your nose because seeds go up it," he said. I asked him what would he suggest? "A nose plug!" Taylor didn't win even though he downed almost a pound and a half in the allotted time. A 10 year-old girl beat him out with a few more ounces bitten out of her slice. Ten year-old Tarnetta Grace took off with her $25 prize to find some souvenirs.

Finding souvenirs is not a hard thing to do when you walk around Cordele. Everything has a green and red touch to it—birdhouses, pottery, and jewelry. Nothing is safe from folks painting seeds on the side.

Cordele folks have Southern hospitality so they figure you can spend your money on stuff besides the actual watermelons. They give free slices away in yellow and red!

As you might expect seed spitting contests reign supreme in this town and they even crown a Watermelon Capitol Queen for the occasion. I figured a queen should be knowledgeable about her subjects but the 2002 tiara-wearing teenager Jessica Overstreet told me, "you don't really have to know anything about watermelons." A perk to the crown is getting to eat watermelon whenever you get a craving. I asked what if you wanted a slice at three o'clock in the morning? "They wouldn't have to get me one but they're so nice they probably would," she said. It figures, after all as Tracy Byrd says, "Well if you're ever down in Georgia round about July, If you ain't in a hurry then you oughta stop by."

....

Logistics:

When: Exact Festival dates change year to year so check by calling the Cordele Chamber of Commerce (229-273-1668). Always late June, or early July.

Directions: From Macon, take I-75 South to Exit 101. Take a right off the ramp and go to 7th Street. Hang a right (Hwy 41) until you hit downtown Cordele.

Circle of Drummers

Indian Dancer in full native costume

Ocmulgee Indian Festival

E very third weekend in September just as the corn crop
has finished its run, people with American roots deeper
than most come to Macon to share their heritage.

The Ocmulgee Indian festival draws native Americans
from five different tribes. The Creek, whose ancestors hunted
and lived on the Ocmulgee Indian ground land, the Cherokee,
the Choctaw, the Chickasaw, and the Seminole.

The tribes invite people to share their heritage, culture,
and way of life. Inside the park you'll see men like Whagoo-Le
dancing to the rhythmic beat of a native drum while shaking
his elaborate body armor made of vibrant reds and yellows.

Another man sits under the shade of a tree in a folding
chair, arrowheads scattered around his feet. He shares insight
of where the pointed treasures came from. He tells the crowd

dogwood was the material of choice for Indians in the Southern Plains.

Kids can learn how native Americans used clay to make ornate pieces of art. This is a hands-on place where putting gooey fingers to the test is all part of the fun. The kids seem to like creating little pinch pots and spiders. At the end of the day they scurry over to pick up the handmade souvenirs.

And just as popular as kids with clay is an adult with a credit card. Yes, shopping is part of this experience! And it runs the gamut from inexpensive beads and drums to wonderfully detailed drawings and authentic buffalo hides and skulls. Just outside one of the stands that had cds and cassettes for sale I met Curtis Moore. "I like anything to do with Indians," he said.

Moore's wife is part Blackfoot and Choctaw. But just recently this man discovered his own Native American past. "I traced my heritage," he said. "My Granddaddy was full Cherokee Indian. I never met him though. He's buried somewhere in North Carolina and until this day I don't know where he is." But he can feel his grandfather's presence. Moore is a truck driver and when he puts in the music of his past he can imagine what the land looked like hundreds of years ago. "I can close my eyes and it takes me back to being on the grounds with the people seeing what they see. I guess you could call it daydreaming" he said.

Moore sent me on my way but steered me over to the Buffalo Burger tent. It's there that I met the person with the most ironic tale of the weekend. Chippa Wolf stood doling out lettuce and cheese onto the buffalo burgers. He owns the outfit but here's the surprising part. "When people ask me what a buffalo burger tastes like I can't tell them," he said. "I'm a vegetarian. I've got a big ole buffalo at home named Thunder."

Chippa assured me Thunder would never make it to the grill. As a matter of fact, this slender, soft spoken guy refuses to touch the meat. "My wife eats it and handles it," he said.

Chippa is definitely making a few bucks by charging six dollars a pop for a platter but don't think he doesn't struggle with the situation. "Is this a moral dilemma being here and selling burgers, yes yes yes! " he exclaimed.

A moral dilemma for Chippa but maybe a deeper look inside for all that visit this festival. "They come out of curiosity, moved in a way that you can't find on the radio or television. They're moved by drum and inspiration."

And settled in a woodsy surrounding maybe this is the most basic forms of entertainment passed down through the generations.

Logistics

Location: At the Ocmulgee Indian Mounds, right off Emory Highway in Macon. The celebration is traditionally held the third weekend in September.
Price: There is a fee to get in but parking is free.
Website: www.HolidayDental.com includes information about the festival and as well as other interesting facts.
Phone: Ocmulgee Indian Mounts (478) 752-8257

Charlie Mack in his favorite hat

People walking around the Big Pig Jig

Big Pig Jig

"**Y**ou don't have to say fifty-four miles south of Macon anymore, you just say Big Pig Jig." Bo Carr spoke to me while overlooking the people's choice awards at one of the biggest barbeque contests in the South. Every year in October a handmade shantytown comes alive in Vienna, Georgia, with 124 teams in place to host the Super bowl of sauce and savory meat. Add some entertainment and an arts and crafts fair and you have quite an event. One woman explained the essence of the Big Pig Jig, "There's not a lot of places you can tote a beer around and ride a Ferris wheel." The place is a compilation of backyard warriors and corporate teams ready to put on the best spread. But before they light the grills they have to come up with names and they run the gamut—Prime Time Swine, Pig-N-Heat, Roasting Roasters, Ham Hock Jocks, Hole Hawg, or Nutin, and Meatslangers, just to name a few.

If you go by the Mack Pigs post you can get a bit of history from Charlie Mack. He's an old timer, one of the original guys to play a part in the contest that started in 1982. Things looked different then. Instead of big fancy black smokers the teams stretched their wire flatbed grills over the ground. "We used to use a bucket and sauce it with a rag and a stick," he said.

Over the years Mack recruited a good bit of his family to swab the shoulders. His brother got a little piggy and broke away from the barnyard to form his own team. "Thought he was better than us but just look out front." Charlie's referring to all of the pigs sitting on top of trophies that *his* teams cooked up.

The teams grill up a lot during the Big Pig Jig run. And as you walk around the rustic place you can see the intensity in their eyes and the sweet smell of success in the air. But a word to the wise, if you go in as a hungry spectator looking to go hog wild *you might find yourself squealing with disappointment.*

"People come out here and they don't realize they can't get the barbeque. You got to have an in to eat." said Carr. Remember she was manning the people's choice booth. It's a new way to get everyone involved if you can't schmooze your way in to a team meal. For a dollar you get to sample twenty-four entries and choose which one tempts your taste buds. Now don't get me wrong, this is a great thing to experience and cooks will give you grilling tips for your own backyard barbeque but don't expect them to give away any secrets. After all, they've got to sow their reputations!

....

Logistics

The Big Pig Jig falls on the second or third weekend in October. Check their website for exact dates.

Website: www.bigpigjig.com

Directions: Vienna is right off Exit 109 on Interstate 75. The entrance to the Big Pig Jig is about a quarter of a mile west of the exit.

Cost: Parking is free but it will cost you a few bucks to get in the door.

Camellia in bloom

Festival of Camellias

Between January and March the colors of a southern garden fade with the winter doldrums. But one flower thrives during the dreary days and come February it puts on a colorful show.

Massee Lane gardens in Fort Valley is home to the American Camellia Society and 2000 different plants over 160 acres.

"There's a lot to see." Anne Walton is the head of Massee Lane. She admits she loves to spend time in the garden but didn't think it would evolve into this. You see Anne is from England, but one trip to the states can change the course of a lifetime. "I came to visit and stayed. I loved the weather." She's now a camellia convert, rattling off trivia like camellias come in six major forms and originated in China, but her favorite flower is magnolia flora. "It's translucent, china-like with a little blush," she explained.

The Festival of Camellias runs throughout the month of February. You can check out all kinds of activities like seminars on pruning and propagating, tours through the gardens, and even a fashion show. Anne says there is another reason folks flock here from all over the states. "Lots of people come to buy. They just tote them out of here." she said.

They wouldn't have that opportunity to tote if it weren't for one man. Non-history buffs can skip to the bottom of the page, but here's a little background for everyone else on how this flower bloomed in Georgia. Camellia japonicas came to America in 1797 or 1798 (when it's that far back who's counting?) when John Stevens of Hoboken New Jersey imported one from England. (It all gets confusing because Camellias are descendants from China.) Anyway by the early 1800s you could pick up the flowers in a lot of cities— Savannah, Charleston, Mobile, New Orleans, etc. After the Civil war folks had more important things to think about besides camellias, so their popularity faded. Then they bloomed back to life in the 1920s. Eventually all of the flower fans got together and formed the Camellia Society. In 1965, David Strother offered to donate his camellia garden, a pecan grove, and farming land in Peach and Macon Counties to the Society. Strother had all of this land that he loved but he never lived on the property. He visited his gardens everyday. The Society accepted Strother's offer and Massee Lane came into existence.

Tom Johnson is the place's horticulturist. He's not old enough to have known David Strother but he did work at Massee Lane as a kid. "Yeah, they made me pull up all the weeds." That weed pulling paid off. Tom grew to love plants and put in a good many years at the Carter Center Gardens in downtown Atlanta. When the opportunity for a horticulturist came up in Fort Valley he had a talk with his wife who is a floral designer and had a good career going in Atlanta. "She put her career on hold to come play Camellia with me." Tom says working at Massee Lane is a way for him to give back to the area where he grew up and he figures he'll retire on this land, but he does miss a certain aspect to his former job. "There is nothing like getting a phone call that says, please hold for the President!"

Yea, that's definitely a tough one to beat, but check out Massee Lane gardens, soak in the color, and enjoy the flower that started as a tourist and planted roots in Central Georgia.

Logistics

Festival of Camellias runs throughout the month of February, but the gardens are open year round. When it's not camellia time on the clock you can enjoy their collection of daylilies, roses, the water garden, or the Boehm Porcelain Collection (This is one of the largest collections in the world. They're fascinating sculptures of mostly birds.) In December, Massee Lane also puts on a festival of trees.
Website: www.Camellias-acs.org.
Phone: Massee Lane Gardens (478) 967-2358
Directions: From Macon go south on I-75, get off on exit 149 and take a right. That will put you on highway 49. Motor on down all the way through Fort Valley and just outside of town you'll see the gardens on your left.

John and Elsie Daniels

Redneck Windchines

Forsythia Festival

It doesn't take much to start a tradition and in this case the Forsythia festival began after a group of good folks wanted to do something special for their town.

"Elaine Treadwell called me up on one day and asked me if I would serve on the board." That happened sixteen years ago explained Connie Ham. And the board Elaine asked Connie to serve on was for the fledgling Forsythia Festival. Ham says Treadwell thought the town needed something positive because Tift College had just closed down. That festival came together and now every year in the middle of March when the forsythia bush turns yellow people in Monroe County celebrate. Connie says the plant, the city, and the festival just seemed to go hand in hand. "She (Elaine) said it's just kind of easy to say Forsyth and forsythia, plus it's native to this area and she would wear yellow before Carolyn Crayton ever thought of wearing pink," Connie said with a smile. (See p. 155 on Crayton and pink).

Now with about a decade and a half under its belt the Forsythia Festival isn't the biggest celebration in Georgia, but every year that goes by another event goes into the books. Over about a week span you can enjoy concerts, a chili cook off, a five-kilometer run and a classic car show but the event that really brings in the crowds is the arts and crafts festival. Vendors from all over come in and nestle into a cozy atmosphere around the classic town square. "Everything has to be handmade. Nothing can be manufactured," said Connie. Because of that hard and steadfast rule you'll find unusual stuff, like hand created redneck wind chimes, burn-you-off-your-seat barbeque sauce and all kinds of paintings and pottery, sweets, and soaps. I even heard one woman serving fruity drinks with a recipe that only her Chihuahua knows! But since it's the Forsythia Festival one guy makes sure you can get your green thumb on the plants themselves.

You can find John and his wife Elsie Daniels sporting bright yellow jackets in the Lions Club booth. John grows Forsythia's like crazy and sells a good many of them at the arts and crafts fair. "It's hardy, easy to grow, always blooms and it stays in bloom ten days to two weeks," he said proudly. If you stop here be prepared to talk, especially if you have any kind of a green thumb. You see John spent many a year as the county extension agent in Monroe County. He likes the forsythia bush but he'll also get you to share his passion for the Cherokee rose, but that's another subject. As for the Forsythia bush, I asked him how he got the job of bringing in all of the yellow plants. That's when one lady shouted "he didn't learn how to say No!" I think it played out a little differently. "Maybe I was just the obvious choice, being a county agent, and I volunteered," he said. Yeah, that will do it, so now John and Elsie, who says she does all the cooking and lets John play with the plants, have an entire room off the basement in their house devoted to cuttings.

Maybe it's folks like the Daniels or maybe it's because the whole thing started out of good will but the Forsythia Festival has an intimate feel to it. I think Elsie described it best. "You meet all sorts of people you don't know and they speak to you. It's a small town atmosphere but it brings in people from all over and those people are accepted as hometown folks."

You have to think that's what Elaine Treadmill would have wanted. She's moved away now, but Connie says as long as she's got anything to do with it the Forsythia Festival will bloom every year, "Till they take me down to Spanky Becks, which is the funeral home!"

Logistics

When: Middle March

Website: www.forsythiafestival.com

Directions: Forsyth is in Monroe county. Coming from Macon, head up I-75 north towards Atlanta. Forsyth is the next town up, about twenty minutes away. The festival is downtown on the square.

Kay looking out over the games

Tools of the trade!

Culloden Games

If you have a tendency to snicker at men in skirts make sure you stay clear of Culloden, Georgia, in April! That's when the little town with a population of a couple hundred swells and bursts its borders to welcome a couple thousand in for the Highland Games.

The games stand as a test of physical strength and a weekend celebration of Scottish culture. Culloden is a natural spot in Central Georgia to have the event since a Scotsman, William Culloden, founded the little town back in the 1780s.

The athletes challenge gravity, hurling archaic chunks of stone. It reminds you of something you might have seen in the days of Fred Flintstone in Bedrock! There is even a complete language to pick up. The Caber toss is probably the most impressive. That's when a telephone looking piece of wood goes flipping through the air. The sheaf toss demands the Scots dig in with a pitchfork and hurl heavy bags of hay over a football like goalpost. And as if that's not enough to wear you out, the competitors do chunk around dead weight, attached by chains, just for fun.

A big hulking mountain of a guy named Kay started the tradition in Culloden with his wife Susan (they married after knowing each other for three days, now they've celebrated 38 years together). Kay is a big name in Highland competitions. He holds some records and if you just look at him the big guy commands respect in his own way. "I'd tell people I'm going to compete in the Highland Games and they didn't know what I was talking about. They thought I was going to play softball." There is nothing soft about this guy or this event, in fact Kay played a part in making sure the competitors who win here walk away with a big prize—a claymore. It's a huge sword and folks feel pretty strongly about winning one. "I got a call from a woman in Scotland and she asked me if I make sword Coozies." Alex Ian Cameron handmakes the claymores and it turns out the woman who wanted the coozie was married to a man who slept with one of Cameron's creations. And although the sword maker travels all over the world the Highland Games in Culloden rank as one of his favorites. "I love this little town. I want to take it back to Florida with me."

Even if you don't toss around the heavy sports equipment it's a lesson in history to go to Culloden at this time of the year. These people are very proud of their heritage. As you walk the streets you'll see men camping out in tents like the olden days (or maybe it's just their wives wouldn't let them back home after a night of Whiskey tasting in the old school house, that happens over the weekend!) Impromptu dancing breaks out with bagpipes providing the music. The Scots trot out some border collies for a professional working dog demonstration, they run around and herd sheep. There is a completely different area for folks to walk around and enjoy Scottish culture. Rows and rows of tents with names like Clan Gregor and Clan Sutherland invite you to stop in and find out if you have a little Scot in ye-self! "When people look up a name in these tents their face lights up, I've seen some of the women squeal," said Kay.

You may replace that squeal for a scream when you get a load of the Scottish snack of choice. It's called Haggis, and it looks like a big meatball. "It's sheep's liver, oats, onions and spices. Wayne and Debbie Mowat have a little concession stand and they admit non-Scots look at them a little strangely after they read the menu. "If you like liver, you might like it. If you don't like liver there's no-way," said Wayne. "Or you know if you don't have enough courage, you can go to the beer tent and then stop by!" If Haggis doesn't float your claymore just grab a fried Mars bar. I asked Wayne about that treat's Scottish history. "I think a woman from Scotland put it on the internet" Hmmm—well maybe, but whether you go for the cuisine or the camaraderie or to earn a claymore check out Culloden. It's the best time of the year to learn about ye Scottish history.

....

Logistics

When: The Culloden games fall on the third weekend in April.
Phone: (478) 885-2440
Directions: From Macon go West on Highway 74 until you come to the intersection and caution light at Highway 341. Take a left and take the upper fork and then you're in Culloden.

Rebels getting ready for battle

Yankees attaching on the field

Old Clinton War Days

Old Clinton War Days is a weekend when the Civil War comes to life. The whole thing might never have started if the town's historical society wasn't looking for a way to make money in 1974. "We had tried everything," explained Earlene Hamilton. "We sold quilts, barbeque, chicken plates, you name it." Although truth be told Earlene was a kid back then, with grunt duties, but her Mom, Miss Annie as they called her, spearheaded everything. "They used to say, give mamma a telephone and a notepad and she's dangerous." Someone in town suggested the historical society use its *history* to make money by getting together with the 16th Georgia Company G, nicknamed the Jackson Rifles. Together they planned one weekend a year when the South would rise up and do battle against the union in a re-enactment of a couple of key fights. The fights never really happened in Clinton but the town did sit on the direct line of the notorious March by Sherman to the sea and federal troops occupied the town in July of 1864 and again in November of the same year. The Yankees left their mark by burning a good bit of the land when they left. After the War Between the States Clinton, which once stood as a booming part of the state, never recovered.

Today Clinton is a small village, but the first weekend of every May the troops move back in. In 1983 when it started they had ironically 83 re-enactors, now that number is pushing 400. "We had to start limiting the Calvary in the field," said Hamilton, "one year a horse got loose, we caught him on highway 129 at the convenience store!" Besides horses stopping for a soda, the confrontations play out in a realistic atmosphere complete with costumes, scouts in the saddle, and gunpowder. As the audience lines the field you can hear the commands of the troops as they creep along in the grass and march on each other—phrases like, "Over the hill, over the hill, get down, they're coming in" or "come on boys, get on the line, get up." But maybe the thing that really puts you in the time frame is the booming cannons that go off. The earth shakes, and the folks jump, except the soldiers who keep on ducking and firing. The gunpowder smoke permeates the air as kids and adults look on in awe and try to relive how life played out on a battlefield.

"People have no idea the scale of the war between the states," said Ricky A. Smith. This scruffy guy dressed in a worn tattered and pinned together uniform travels all around the country to play a part in civil war re-enactments. For him the passion started as a kid. "1965 commemorated the 100 year anniversary of the civil war," he explained, "these bubblegum cards came out with civil war scenes on them and I just about wore out my jaws chewing so much gum." The spark took and as he grew up he traced some of his relatives who played a part in the war. "They were in the 27th Georgia out of Crawford county," he said. Smith says there is a lot of appeal in dressing in stifling hot costumes and crawling around in a field with gunpowder filling up your nostrils. "You hear the civil war accounts of how hard it was to push the enemy back a couple of miles and in re-enacting you understand. It's totally exhausting fighting in 100 degree weather. I've seen some men so dehydrated they have to leave the field but they have tears in their eyes."

That's a lot of emotion and before the battle begins a narrator takes folks through what kind of things happened in the 1800s, how they fought, what they thought and strategy along the lines. "Re-enactors say this isn't the largest one in the country but it's one of the best and one of the reasons is the narration in the beginning," said Hamilton. "If you're not into civil war history you don't really know what you're looking at." Hamilton says if you go, check out the battles but definitely carve out time for the memorial service that happens Saturday night. That's when the unit dressed in full uniform and accompanied by a woman dressed in black widow's attire march to the cemetery. Smith usually gives the eulogy and a poet reads what he's written during the weekend. They take roll call with a soldier standing at each gravesite with a candle and when a name is called the soldier replies "present in spirit, sir" and he extinguishes his flame. "It just grabs at your heartstrings," said Hamilton.

These days Hamilton herself has some sore heartstrings. Miss Annie passed away in 2003 at the age of 84. And now the notepad and the telephone are the responsibility of her daughter. "It takes a lot to put it on, but I guess it's in my blood." Just like a lot of the folks carrying on their heritage on and off the field.

Logistics

When: The first weekend of May

Directions: From Macon head down old Clinton highway towards Gray. It's twelve miles northeast of Macon and one and a half miles southwest of Gray. Just outside Gray you'll see signs directing you to turn left. Parking is in a field right outside the village.

Cost: $5 for adults and $3 for kids.

Phone: Earlene Hamilton, (478) 986-6383

Extras: An arts and crafts show and folks called *suttlers* (storekeepers) who sell civil war clothes and memorabilia. The re-enactors also set up authentic tent camps where they live for the weekend and you're welcome to walk through, look, and strike up a conversation!

Vat of Peach Cobbler

Carol and Diane Barrett show off their peach headgear

Peach Festival

You got to figure with Georgia affectionately called the peach state the folks in Peach County, have their work cut out for them to live up to the title. Well, they do try to accomplish things in a big way. Every year folks come from all over to try some of the self proclaimed Worlds Largest Peach cobbler, (it's self proclaimed because of some snafu with Guinness. Seems the world record holder doesn't keep track of fruit.) "It's ninety pounds of butter, thirty two gallons of milk, one hundred and fifty pounds of flower, two hundred and fifty pounds of sugar and fifteen 5-gallon buckets of Georgia peaches." Matt Mullis can rattle off the mammoth recipe without any trouble. Dressed in flip-flops, a visor, and a sunburned face, the main cook says he's in his fifth year conjuring up the cobbler. It's a process that defies anything Martha Stewart has in her kitchen! "First we mix the flour and sugar in a trash can," explained

Matt. "Then we use a garden rake as a sifter to get all the lumps out of it." Matt says once they have the batter together they pour in the peaches into the 11 by 5 foot vat. Pretty simple stuff, but over the years folks have told him he needs to add one ingredient. "They say put in nutmeg, but naaaa."

It goes over without the spice. A line wraps around the shelter built especially for this event. Serving starts at about four o'clock Saturday afternoon. And as folks step up to the plate for a four-ounce cup with sticky stuff dripping over the sides, they do make their requests for special spaces. "They'll ask you for the peaches part, or they'll ask for the crust." Eugenia Wood doesn't like cobbler, but for the last fifteen years she's leaned over the huge sweet treat to dollop out the goo. This good-natured woman does have fun with some of the folks. "One person asked me how many pounds of dirt did we put in it, and I told them oh, about three and a half pounds!"

Hard to find that sand, the cobbler tossed with garden tools is surprisingly creamy and the warm gooey crust is pretty gummy and delicious.

Charles Holsey was born and raised in the peach belt, and the guy has eaten his fair share of cobbler in his lifetime. "I love what they do with the peaches, but no one can come close to my mother's or my wife's cobbler, but it's good!" Holsey finished his cup pretty quick. Seems he was afraid his wife or mother might pick up this book! Anyway the cobbler takes center stage but the peach festival is chock full of other peachy activities. Some of the local grower's truck in big bins right out of the field that folks can pick through (and boy do they pick through) and take home a free sack of peaches. There is entertainment like dancers that encourage people to step forward and do a little booty shaking. And vendors that encourage you to take home everything from jewelry to birdhouses, all of course with the state theme engrained in one way or another.

And Saturday night when the headline band steps off the stage they don't get any midnight snacks from the vat. Matt says every year towards the end of the festival people scrape the sides filling up their Tupperware with the cobbler to preserve a little bit of the festival for a few more days. "Yea, by eight or nine o'clock there is very little left in that thing." Until next year when the rakes and trash cans come out of the closet to make maybe the most unknown, world's-largest cobbler!

Logistics

When & Where: The second weekend in June. Events are held in Byron and Fort Valley (Peach County). The parade is Saturday morning and the World's Largest Peach Cobbler is made Saturday afternoon in Fort Valley.

Directions: Coming from Macon follow I-75 south to Byron, exit 149. From Byron, take GA Highway 49, about 12 miles to downtown Fort Valley.

Website: www.gapeachfestival.com

Phone: (877) 322-4371

Working Blacksmith

Helen Cannon
putting together
her brooms

Mossy Creek
Barnyard Festival

S pring and fall in Central Georgia is a time when a
flurry of festivals hit the calendar. If you long for the
simple days of farm life when people shoed their
horses and kids played with pop guns hiding behind trees
you can't miss the Mossy Creek Barnyard Festival. The whole
thing is set in a dense forest of trees. As the sunlight filters
through the trees people sell their wares. You'll find
blacksmiths carving out iron sculptures, potters, painters,
jewelry makers, and everything in between.

A spry 81-year-old woman and her husband started this
bi-annual event. Carolyn Chester always loved arts and crafts
festivals. Before she retired from Northside High School as
the librarian, she and her friend would go around visiting
different events. Carolyn and her husband E. B. decided to
stage their own in 1981. They had the land, they just needed

the experience. They went with a fall date on the calendar. "When we started in '81 it rained the total time," Carolyn says. "We were discouraged but the exhibitors weren't, so we had one in the spring!"

It still rains every now and then but the event blossomed and now 150 exhibitors come to town to sell their stuff to the thousands of folks who pass through the wooden gates. It's invitation only, so 150 get chosen to come. Carolyn estimates 20-30 new ones each festival.

"People are so interested, at most festivals they just walk by, here they stop and talk to you and the setting is so gorgeous." Helen Cannon is one of the few Georgia artists that got the lucky invitation in the mail. She makes brooms, but not the kind of brooms you would pull out of the closet. These you might want to display. Each one has a personality, whether it's a knarled handle, or especially hand picked hay, Helen spends a good bit of time on these sweepers. "I go out and find sticks and wood on construction sites or wherever they take down trees, I really get a bigger kick out of that than making the brooms." She can't help the need to weave the strands together. "My Daddy was a broom maker. I wanted to learn but he wouldn't teach me. He said it wasn't very ladylike."

Helen is more ladylike at this festival than a lot of women. Walking by you see a lot of the artists dressed in early American style, complete with long dresses and bonnets for the women, suspenders and long white shirts for the men. "We don't insist that they do that, we want everyone to be happy." Carolyn said. And this lady who spends the whole year working for two weekends thinks people are happy. She reads about it in the guest book. "One lady from Miami said it's like an enchanted forest. I think the friendliness helps make it enchanted."

Enchanted might be a good term. Where else can you hear a dulcimer player while checking out handmade clay houses, sing with the Sweet Adelaines (Acapulco ladies group) while licking hand churned ice cream, tap your toes to Bluegrass just before you hit an old timer up for some fishing tips that you'll use with your new handmade pole, take a hayride, then catch a clogging show? It all happens on 12 acres. Check it out. After all the kingdom comes to life rain or shine!

Logistics

When: The Mossy Creek Barnyard Festival happens the third weekend in October and the third weekend in April. (The April date moves if it happens to fall on Easter weekend.)
Phone: (478) 922-8265
Website: www.mossycreekfestival.com
Directions: From Macon take 1-75 to exit 142 which is GA 96. From there follow the signs to the festival. It's located four miles from Perry.
Admission: At the time of this writing the fee at the gates was five dollars with free parking.

Free Cherry Ice Cream served up every day in the park

Cherry Blossoms bursting on the trees

Cherry Blossom

Every spring when the air flutters with the first signs of warmth and the trees wake up from their sleepy winter slumber an event that's come to define a town happens in Macon.

People come from all over the Southeast and all over the world to enjoy, play a part, and soak in the Cherry Blossom Festival.

The ten day event which hosts hundreds of events with a large portion not costing folks a dime started out as a humble expression of gratitude to a man who brought some unusual greenery to the area. "I started it to say thank you to Mr. Fickling for the trees." Carolyn Crayton is an icon in this town, a woman who rarely wears anything but pink, and a passionate spirit that's grown the festival into an event that gets national attention. But that took time and it also took a man by the name of William A. Fickling Sr. to find a cherry blossom tree in his yard. Its foliage gives off big, poofy pink and white clustery flowers in the spring and stays hearty and green the rest of the year. By the early 1950s Fickling figured out a way to propagate the showy tree and share the saplings with all of his neighbors. Crayton came up with the weekend celebration to thank the Fickling's for their generosity and to give away more trees. "The first one we gave away 30-thousand trees and now we've given away 285 thousand trees."

And now those thousands of trees provide a picturesque backdrop for everything that surrounds the Cherry Blossom Festival. You can spend hours in Central City park walking around the booths, hearing performers on stage and of course getting your fill of fair food. At night the Ocmulgee Indian mounds open up for flashlight led walks. Giant hot air balloons take off one weekend and light up the night before in a balloon glow celebration. Folks dress in poodle skirts and high stepping shoes for the sixties dance. Two parades full of all kinds of floats and bands march down the streets. All kinds of creative folks line Second Street for an arts and crafts festival and the list goes on and on.

Crayton enjoys it all but says special guests coming into town give the festival a special flair. "We have Ambassadors, Lords and Ladies, and Consul Generals. We even got the Welch Guard to come but first we had to get the Queen's permission." On any given afternoon you may also enjoy the sounds of Japanese Demon Drummers, or hear members of the Belfast Ireland male choir. Crayton believes in the international invitations to promote goodwill. After all the Cherry Blossom did originate in Japan, but now the American

Congressional record names Macon, Georgia as the Cherry Blossom capitol of the world. And it's all the greenery, or maybe I should say pinkery that touches the heart of the woman who started it all. "To me what makes it so special are the flowers of the trees whether it's in the city, the county, the industrial area or in any neighborhood. I don't believe you can go anywhere and not see a tree."

And corporate America has taken notice, Coca-Cola released two Cherry Blossom bottles and Crayton even convinced Sweet and Low to stamp the logo on their pink packets. The queen of marketing is working on Crayola to put out a Cherry Blossom pink crayon. "I think they should because we do a sidewalk chalk with the children." Even if the crayon company doesn't come around Crayton knows she's done what many of us want to do, leave something behind that will always live in the hearts of Maconites. "It's just overwhelming and humbling and it's certainly been a great joy to see the festival become very successful and I love the fact that Macon is known for something really positive." Really positive and really pink. It's a combination that's a spark of something to look forward to every spring in the south.

....

Logistics

Website: www.cherryblossom.com
Phone: (478) 751-7429
Festival Dates: The festival usually falls towards the end of March depending on the Easter schedule. Call or check the website for specific dates each year.

CHAPTER 4

Places

*Sometimes you never know
what to expect from an adventure.
It's one of those unique experiences
that doesn't fit in a category.*

The view inside

Jean Hansgen at home in the shop

Harmonious Balance

The motto for this little shop in Ingleside Village is "In this hectic world you deserve some Harmonious Balance." "Every now and then someone comes in with the deer in the headlights look. Its so different it just rocks their world." Jean Hansgen owns and runs the shop that's full of everything from chanting music to lingering incense. You can find the perfect crystal for a friend or peruse the rows and rows of books on religion and self help. Stones from Peru and China sit on the shelves, as do many different awareness cards. This is also a place where you can read a little Zen or find out about Feng Shui. A couple of times a month Jean lets folks come on in and just pound on the drums. "She says it's therapeutic and can lower your blood pressure."

She should know. This short yet opinionated woman didn't began her career wanting to run a shop. She started as a nurse. "I was depressed and it just sort of came to me, totally do something different."

When you spend time with Jean she talks about positive energies and the spiritual side of life, and whereas she knows not everyone will take a liking to the clothes from Nepal or run in for the Olive Oil shampoo she does think folks could find something of interest. "Depending on what people think it may or may not be what I believe or think, it's not for me to judge. In fact it's more illuminating to see the things we have in common. I want everyone to feel special because they are."

Felicia Hammett feels pretty special when she comes in. "It always smells better than my house," she said with a smile. "The crystals are just like a magnet. I go right to them. If I'm close, I'll stop by. I've spent godzoodles of time here."

Jean doesn't care how much time you spend. As a matter of fact she says a lot of folks come in just to get away and take a break from the outside world. "After 9-11 a lot of people came in and they didn't come to buy, they came here to sit and be peaceful. We're too caught up with business. We all need to nourish ourselves more. I try not to be busy if I can help it. I quit wearing a watch years ago."

She may have to abandon the time piece but she does realize the enjoyment she gets out of this time in her life. "This pleases me very much, I'm much poorer financially but richer spiritually."

Logistics

Where: 2326 Ingleside Avenue

Directions: From Macon, go down Riverside Drive and turn onto Ingleside Avenue. (You can only turn one way from Riverside Drive.) Drive through the neighborhood until you come to Ingleside Village. Harmonious Balance is on your left.

Phone: (478) 742-3196

Website: www.harmoniousbalance.com

Outside of Lawrence Mayer's Florist

Roses inside the cooler

Lawrence Mayer Florist Shop

It's funny how we start out as kids thinking we'll go in one direction and then turn out to work at something completely different in our lives. Case in point Lawrence Mayer, "Went to college to be a biochemist. I hated chemistry," the gentle flower man said with a grin. "How I got talked into that I'll never know."

So the guy who didn't like formulas and periodic tables looked for something else to do. "My father's sister was a garden editor for the Detroit news. She said, "you've always loved flowers," and thus a career and a legacy was born. Mayer started his flower shop in Detroit, but in a region where things depend on cars the business just didn't grow in the 1980s. "When the car business has a cough, everyone else has pneumonia" he said. To heal his virus Mayer moved to Macon in 1983, after he checked out the place on a trip visiting a friend. "People didn't have an opportunity to buy flowers here; back then they had to go to a wholesaler," he explained.

Of course in twenty years times have changed and folks who love flowers can get them almost anywhere, but Lawrence Mayer and his Disneyland like shop have built up a reputation in town. "This is a destination store, people come here that don't go to other stores in town." Well it is a unique experience. When you walk into the historic cornerstone place soothing music drifts through the air, thanks to an automatic playing baby grand in the middle of the shop. Besides colorful, fragrant, and striking blooms on display in the coolers, you can also buy pottery, houseplants, candy, and cards. A simple bunch of daisies might run you five bucks, but the more unusual flowers can run the gamut on price. "Every flower that's available in the world, you can get here," he chuckled, "well not every one but almost!" That list does include Hyacinths from Holland, Orchids from Thailand or Delphiniums from Ecuador.

At the age of 73, Mayer comes to work everyday but now he tends to supervise. He has made quite a few arrangements in his lifetime. The artist says Macon has its own style. "In the north it was more contemporary. We'd have potters come in just to make special containers, he explained. "An arrangement of all Bird of Paradise would be too contemporary for Macon, but up north it's an everyday staple."

Mayer and his shop have become an everyday staple in Macon, he has passed the business down to his son Jonathan (just call him a petal off the old blossom). And maybe life didn't turn out too bad for a chemist who figured out a colorful equation for happiness.

....

Logistics:

Phone: (478) 743-0221
Where: Located at 608 Mulberry Street in downtown Macon, Georgia.

Bee's buzzing
around their box

John with fresh bee granules

Bees

When you drive down highway 49 just out of Milledgeville you might bee tempted to take a double take at a little house on the road. In the yard you'll see colorful drawers stacked four and five apiece upon each other. The guy's got dozens of them filled with creatures earning their humble keep. John Pluta panders to some unusual tenants—bees! It's actually a business that began out of necessity. "I was farming fruit and I needed the bee's to pollinate," explained Pluto. "I didn't want them and I didn't want to know about them. I even put them in a back area of my field. I figured they might kill me and I didn't want them around the house." But the bees didn't kill him and then the fine art of capitalism came calling. "Well this couple came by and they wanted a beehive. I made a quick profit and thought hmmm, there might *be* something to this."

Now the guy has four hundred hives around the state including 120 in Central Georgia. Pluta sells the bees but he also sells all kinds of products from the flying insects. You can buy honey pecan brittle, honeycombs, bees wax, beeswax chews, and pollen energy granules. Yes, energy granules. Pluta who buzzes around like an energetic bee himself says he takes a spoonful everyday. "They're pure protein with a sweet nutty taste; it's the stuff the bees feed the babies in the hive. We just catch it by making the bee's walk over a grate and it falls through."

Pluta keeps most of the loot down by the road and away from the hives. It turns out bees can get a might ornery. Pluta says they tend to sting more if the sun doesn't come out. With testy insects buzzing around you don't want folks walking through the yard. You definitely take your chances if you wander. "On a good day I'll only get twenty stings or so." I asked him what a bad day looked like. Pluta told me more than twenty.

Pluta's patient. You have to be when working with bees. But the guy does have fun with people who stop by. As Pluta and I stood in the yard, ironically a gentleman ran out of gas right in front of the place.

Kerry Pearson is a big, athletic-looking type and after he figured where his misfortunes dropped him the first words out of the guy's mouth were, "they don't sting do they?" Pluta soothed Pearson's paranoia and sent him on his way with gas and a couple of honey sticks, but don't be surprised if the bee master gives you a dare.

"Yeah, I'll tell people if they stick their hand in the hive it's a dollar less, kind of pick it yourself," Pluta chuckled and said most everyone opts to pay the extra buck!

So maybe you don't want to hike through the hives, but do ask to see John's library. It's a complete collection of beekeeping dating back to the 1800s. Research is how he learned all of the interesting facts about bees. For example women rule in the bee world, each hive is about 99 percent female, and each one of Pluta's boxes holds about 20-thousand renters.

So if you have a craving for a sweet treat or you want to light up your world with a beeswax candle, just pull off the side of the road. John will bee sure to show you around his world that's positively benign with the buzzing creatures.

Logistics

Directions: Pluta's place is right off Highway 49 just outside of Milledgeville. You'll see the signs outside his house on the right hand side of the road.

Times: John works hives all over the state but he says he's usually at home and ready to sell honey Friday through Sunday.

Extras: If you want to get into farming bees John does sell the hives and the much sought after queen bee for $12. You can also buy wax in bulk.

Phone: (478) 452-2337

Ray getting ready to shoot

Shooter on the range

Cowboy Gun Slingers

I first met Ray Ryals while waiting for my table at a
steakhouse in Warner Robins. Among folks sporting
summertime shorts and polos this guy sat at the bar
decked out in full cowboy regalia—hat, holster, bandana,
and boots—the works. After I chuckled a little and thought
what's up with this guy, I got to talking to him and he
shared with me all about a club he started back in 1996, the
Lonesome Valley Regulators, which is part of the single
action shooting society.

So the next time these cowboys and girls got together, I
showed up too and I found myself spending an afternoon
straight out of a scene in the 1800s Wild West.

Men and women, cowboys, and even a couple of Indians
step up to wooden backdrops for a pretend or simulated
Hollywood gunfight. They never take aim at each other. It's
more of a sharp shooter square off. They let loose with lead

bullets against steel targets in pistol, rifle, and shotgun competition and the whole thing makes quite a racket. It sounds and looks like something you would have seen about 100 years ago on a dusty town road. Imagine the gunpowder smell in the air and loud clangs and booms ricocheting through your ears. The whole thing made me duck behind a barrel! When I caught a little courage I moseyed on over to one of the women in the group, Alice Rye—otherwise known as Dallas. Alice looked lovely, yet intimidating at the same time. She showed up in a period correct green dress, accessorized by a hulking strap of green shot gun shells wrapped around her waist! "It's a totally new world people don't know about and it's fun," she said. I never saw Miss Kitty carrying ammunition, but Alice says a woman had to know how to sling lead to survive. So she shoots with her husband and the rest of the boys but admits her real love in Lonesome Valley is the threads. "I love it because of the clothes. I really like dressing up in Victorian dresses."

Ray says the clothes play a big part in lending authenticity to the whole thing; he gains attention out in public much like he caught my eye. And this old timey cowboy does have to deal with some snickering city slickers. "Oh yeah, I get teased, folks saying are you the marshal, want to come and arrest me." Ray, whose buddies call him Dixie Brick, takes it all in stride. "People are rude because you're different, but the point is to give a good image of cowboy shooting."

Ray is all about image because the campfire, stirrups, and
suspenders lifestyle is close to his heart. Every time he steps
up to take aim, the days of yesteryear run through his head.
"It's a chance to play cowboys again. You can relive your
youth." Ray's youth came complete with cowboy movie
matinees on Saturdays and his heroes shooting on *Gunsmoke.*
He loved that time in history and never forgot his days of
shooting cap guns. When he got old enough Ray got paid
for his cowboy dreams working cattle in Montana,
Wyoming, and South Dakota. He's too old now to mix it up
with any frisky bulls these days, but the Lonesome Valley
gives him a place to keep the old way of life alive. "I'm not
terribly fast, I just try to hit the target. I don't really care if I
hit or miss, I just love doing it." And he'd love for you to
come on out and enjoy the show. The curious need not join
the club unless that's what you want. Ray says that across the
nation over five thousand have joined the SAS. But I reckon
out of all those shooters, maybe only a few rival the passion
of a man who lives everyday in the shadow of time. "Even if
I get too decrepit to shoot, I'll still come out!"

Logistics

When: The posse gets together the first Sunday of every
month to shoot 'em out!
Directions: Two and a half miles past the Twiggs county line
on Highway 57.
Phone: (478) 788-3635
Website: www.lrrhomestead.com

SUZANNE LAWLER

Little John's tombstone

Sculpture missing arms

Rosehill Cemetery

I t's easy to assume Rose Hill Cemetery is named after the dozens of colorful roses that line the entrance gates into the historic cemetary. But that's not quite true, the origins of Rose Hill date back to the mid-1800s. Simri Rose sat on the city council back then and he had a vision. Today his dreams of a beautiful meandering natural park-like atmosphere still live right off of Riverside Drive in Macon. Stunning statues patiently sit like skyscrapers guarding the graves across green terraces. "It takes several visits to take it all in." Marty Willett is pretty passionate about these grounds. A few times during the year he leads folks on Rose Hill Rambles and tells the stories behind all the stone.

"Each time you come here it's different, part of that is the eighty acres you might see a new piece of artwork or a flower, there's always something alive." Alive is a word that might seem strange used in a cemetery setting but you've got to think this wasn't designed as just a burial ground. Rose wanted this to also stand as a public park. Marty says back in the early 1900s these grounds filled up with people who used it for social events, like buggy rides and big band concerts. Today mostly joggers and visitors come by. "Some people are just too righteous about the whole thing; why can't you come in here and have a picnic now. Hey if these people could talk they'd say loosen up. Come celebrate my death."

The death and graves of two of the Allman Brother's Band may stand as the most famous sites on the sprawl. Two big white stones lay under a shady tree. "Duane Allman and Berry Oakley both died in two motorcycle wrecks within two blocks of each other" said Marty. And even as we passed through a man decked out in biker gear walked up to quietly pay his respects. Marty says a lot of people stop in Macon just to see the Allman brother's burial plot. But he added these two guys have brought generations together beyond the grave. "Grandparents bring their grandkids here and vice versa."

The Allmans will always attract attention but a lot of Central Georgia history comes with a good many of the plots. You'll find markers for mayors, governors, 600 confederate soldiers, some legislators, a show horse, and two dogs. There is even a nondescript unmarked section of a family killed in a mass murder. The Woolfolk ax murders happened in the late 1800s. "They were a very prominent family ranging in age from 18 months to 80 and they were all axed to death together. They hung Thomas A. Woolfolk, the brother, for the crime," explained Marty. Thomas is buried in Hawkinsville. "People said he did it for the inheritance which didn't make sense because everyone knew the family was broke." More suspicion came down years later when a part-time employee confessed to the murders as he was being lynched for a similar crime.

And speaking of crime, vandals have played a part in the history of Rose Hill too. It's not uncommon to see hands and other pieces of sculpture missing. "One of the worst acts happened when someone stole four marble angles off one monument. That was a professional hit!"

All of the chubby cherubs and tall angelic ambassadors do catch your eye as soon as you set foot into Rose Hill, but Marty says look closely on every tombstone for the words chiseled into the rock. One epitaph reads, "They that saw in tears shall reap in joy." Little John B. Ross Juhan died when he was eight years old. He loved fire engines, so his plot is adorned with a fireman's coat and hat. On the bottom it says, "He was a brave little fireman, attached to the Defiance Fire Co. No. 5."

Simri Rose got to choose the best plot in the place for his afterlife. He picked a spot overlooking the Ocmulgee River. In hindsight, how could this man with so much vision ever contemplate our modern society? You see along with the peaceful flowing waters of the river, Mr. Rose has to contend with the interstate in the background and a rumbling train coming down the tracks a few times a day. "I think he would have chosen a better spot," said Marty. Maybe, but it could be Simri's looking down from above, happy that Rosehill is still an important part of history in his town.

Logistics

Directions: Rose Hill Cemetery is just a few blocks from the intersection of Spring Street and Riverside Drive
Location: 1071 Riverside Drive. **Hours:** 8:30 a.m. to Sunset
Phone: (478) 751-9119
For More Information: Contact Historic Macon (formerly Middle Georgia Historic Society) (478) 743-3851
Warning: The gates to the cemetery close at sundown. I found out the hard way by getting stuck inside. Just park outside the gates and walk in. Believe me, the police won't take kindly to you puttering around after dark!

New Perry Hotel

The New Perry Hotel

At the New Perry Hotel you won't find valet service and they don't keep a concierge on staff. As a matter of fact, they don't even put mints on the pillow! But what you will find will either amaze or anger you. "If we don't tell them in advance they can have a pretty negative reaction." Chuck Linn runs the place and has spent thirty-three years in the hotel business. He's worked at the modern motels, but that came to an end when he came to this property.

When you walk through the doors at the New Perry Hotel you may think it's just a genteel southern place done in soft yellows and greens. The lobby almost has a Florida feel to it with original 1928 furniture. There is a white radiator for heat and an old phone booth in the corner. But it's when you go upstairs to your room the surprise factor starts to kick in. The rooms are small, very small! You won't find tubs, but you will find old timey white tile floors. Chenille bedspreads lay on the beds as a reminder of something your grandmother may have crocheted for the room. It's not all old fashioned, all the rooms have television sets, but you can't make a long distance call. "At that time you just didn't do that from your room," said Chuck.

Some rooms have a balcony to sit on to look over town and other rooms have little sitting areas. Beautiful furniture sits in the hallways but they don't have ice machines. "We have ice cabinets—that is what they had back then—so once a day someone comes up and fills it up with ice." Look out the windows you'll still see the old time fire escapes where you grab hold of the chain to unlock the ladder going down.

"There is a tremendous market for people who want to remember things from 30-40 years ago—they're fascinated."

The New Perry hotel history actually goes back more than forty years ago. "The first building went up on the land in 1822. It served as a stagecoach stop on the way to Florida, but it burned down in the late 1800s," Chuck explained. In 1893, the Perry Hotel opened up but it burned down too. So the New Perry Hotel re-opened in 1928 and the name stuck through the years.

A good many people come for the whole experience but the restaurant also has its own reputation for good southern cooking. Things like country fried steak, slow cooked pot roast, okra and tomatoes, and macaroni and cheese sit on the menu. The waitress will start you off with a relish tray and a bit of soup. Sticking with the historic tradition, a Christmas menu even hangs on the wall from 1933. One lady's built up her own history; Lillie Mae Marchall has worked in the kitchen for thirty years. It's her peach cobbler that has folks making sure they save room for dessert. I asked her for the secret recipe. "I'm not gonna tell you the recipe because you'll tell someone else. I just make it good!"

That's good enough for me and it's good enough for the Kirkpatricks. This couple started coming to the New Perry Hotel back in 1973. "It has class, with fresh linen and fresh flowers, any season of the year," said Shirley. Her husband Bob had his own reasons for keeping the tradition alive. "So many places you go and eat today there is so much racket you can't carry on the conversation, not just the music but the kitchen noise." When Bob's parents come to town, they don't stay at the Kirkpatricks, they go to, you guessed it, the New Perry Hotel. "I think it's more of a thing to say oh, I stayed in the hotel. It's a real tradition for a lot of people. If you have company coming you gotta bring them here," Shirley explained, "usually they'll ask you to anyway."

So check out the New Perry Hotel, a place that's not really new but for many it's a new experience going back in time.

....

Logistics

Where: Downtown Perry at 800 Main Street.
Other Accommodations: If you don't want to stay in the historic hotel you can stay in the modern motel. Both share a pool and a garden to stroll through.
Phone: (800) 877-3779 or (478) 987-1000
Website: www.newperryhotel.com

*Little Miles
and his family*

Planes flying overhead in formation

Warner Robins Air Show

For those of you who don't know, I work in a newsroom. Every now and then a flurry of calls will light up the phones with panicked people complaining of a loud noise that shook the foundations of their homes. It's scary for them, but people who've lived in Warner Robins for awhile know it's only the sonic boom of fighter jets going by.

Every two years the air force base opens its doors and lets people come onto the flight line to see up close and personal what's making the racket in their kitchens and living rooms. The air show is a spectacular event. It's free which is a bonus in itself but it's quite a unique experience to walk beside mammoth buildings called docks that house planes that in some way, shape, or form defend our freedom.

The Air Force's elite fly in to perform, but you also have the chance to look inside cavernous cargo planes, get your picture taken next to a fighter jet, or look over the controls of a K-C 135 refueling plane.

"My dad's retired Army. I came on base when I was knee high to a billy goat." Retired Master Sergeant Jim Howard spent twenty-four years in the ranks, eleven of those years at Robins. He describes the scene as kind of a carnival atmosphere with people camped out on blankets and kids running around with toy airplanes. It's a good feeling for the veteran to see folks appreciating what he's dedicated his life to doing. "To me I think it lets you know where your tax dollars are going and I think it makes people proud, you know the kind of proud that makes the hair on the back of your neck stand up. I know it stands up on the back of my neck."

Every hair on your body can't help but stand at attention when the mighty Thunderbirds take to the air. Remember when I talked about loud noise? The F-16's whizzing by one another at deafening speeds make a fireworks display sound like a golf announcement. (By the way they do give out free earplugs when you come through the gate.) Six year-old Miles Ferguson may describe it best, "I think it's loud, like 2000 percent loud!" Well, when you have six planes performing behind 100,000 pounds of thrust, things can be thunderous (They don't call them Thunderbirds for nothing). The airmen in the cockpit and on the ground are the elite of the Air Force. "There is excellence in everything we do. Not everybody gets to be on this team. The odds are only one out of every 3000." Tech Sergeant Gabriel Quintana beat the odds and travels most of the year with the Thunderbirds. Even though their name headlines any air show in the world,

Quintana says it's what they get back that keeps them performing. "A lot of people will come up to us and thank us for what we do," he said. "Sometimes senior citizens will walk up with tears in their eyes because they've served and it gets really emotional, because we want to say to them 'no, thank *you*' because you laid the ground work for us to be here."

Whether you served, admire the men in blue, or just pay taxes, carve out some time when Robins opens its doors. It's hard not to feel something with the military performing as *Off They Go into the Wild Blue Yonder* plays in the background.

....

Logistics

Directions: Warner Robins Air Force Base is on Highway 247 at the end of Watson Boulevard in Warner Robins.

The air show hits on the calendar every two years. At the time of this book's publication the last show was in 2003.

Website: www.airshownetwork.com

You can find out all about Robins Air Force Base and some of the greatest moments in military flight every day of the year at the Museum of Aviation. It sits adjacent to the base in Warner Robins. They're open everyday of the year 9-5 p.m. except Christmas, Thanksgiving, and New Years Day. Plus it's absolutely free to walk in and check out the exhibits. The place spreads over acres but some of the highlights include the Flying Tigers, the Georgia Aviation Hall of Fame, and the Tuskegee Airmen. You can find out more at their website at www.museumofaviation.org.

SUZANNE LAWLER

Brenda gets the
goodies ready

Ladies enjoying afternoon Tea

Tea in Thomaston

When was the last time you took time in your day to have tea? One woman in Thomaston does everyday; in fact she's built a business around the traditional pastime. "I fell in love with tea time when I was 15." Brenda Rowell said with a reminiscent smile. "As I got older I realized the romance of tea and all the different things that go with tea time." As she got older Brenda also used tea to simmer down after a tough day in the corporate world. On her vacations tea also took center stage along with her love of history. "I would travel when I could and chose a place in the United States—my goal was to see every state capitol— and then I would always search out a tea room." Life went along and then reality hit home. "I almost lost mom in 1999." That got her thinking about life and dreams, so she took an early retirement and set out to find the perfect spot for her business idea that always brewed inside of her. "One day I drove into Thomaston and thought whoa this is it." She fit in her love of history by buying a single story 1820s cottage. Some of the original wood flooring is still in the house. It has a rustic feel that Brenda has accentuated with some antique-like lighting, a couple of dolls, a grandfather clock, and soft music in the background. It's a more feminine feeling with fresh flowers and teapots. Formal place settings sitting on doilies and decked out with fine china accompany the three seating rooms. But a good many of the decorations Brenda *expects* you to take off the wall. When you walk in you can pick out any of the hats, furs, and gloves to adorn your modern clothing. This is a tea party after all and one must look the part and dress up. "Most do, I don't force anybody to dress up, but you're supposed to be young and you'll hear them laughing and being light about it."

On my visit I sat with a group of laughers who probably had ties to the Ya-Ya Sisterhood. The party of six women came to celebrate a birthday. Miss Purl turned ahhh…29. Yea, that's it, 29 and holding right. "I hadn't played dress up in a long time," said Purl. Purl didn't do a lot of tea drinking either. "I never had hot tea before in my life. They asked me about tea and I said I only know about Lipton!" The very stylish women in their own right oohed and ahhed when the first round of snacks hit the table. You can expect a three-tiered tray to come out filled with scones, little sandwiches, and delectable desserts. Don't fight! Brenda stacks one of everything on board for every person along with a generous serving of faux Devonshire cream and lemon curd. She also gives a warning. "Now ladies if you go to any tea room that doesn't offer you a cucumber sandwich you best be investigating!"

You have thirty-three flavors of tea to chose from that mostly come from the West Indies. "Somebody said it was just like Baskin Robins," said Brenda. When the teapot comes out Brenda tells you about the cubes of sugar. Some have little edible flowers sitting on top of the grains. "I suggest two cubes of sugar and milk (whole milk is best for tea). The first glass always comes with a pretty cube. Sometimes it's hard to find a pretty in a day and this way you get one pretty."

The whole experience is pretty wonderful, and I, like Purl, really only knew Lipton before I walked into the cottage. Brenda served everything perfectly. Like the story of Goldilocks and the three bears, I can say the tea was neither too hot nor too cold, but just right. And the tiers left the table empty along with our plates of diced chicken on a crusty croissant with toasted almonds and tomato Napoleon. As for the pseudo-Ya Ya's, "We're gonna have to do this once a month!"

Brenda and her crew will take a snapshot of the party, but it doesn't go home with you, it goes up on the wall. "Sometimes when I might be down I look at those pictures and then I'll go bake some scones." Yes, everything is homemade. And the same light hearted experience that you get Brenda gets as she plays out the second part of her life. "I'll get here early in the morning and start baking, and the birds will sing, the cat comes by (Tea Cup also dines on fine china but on the back porch!) and I'll have my own pot of tea brewing and I'll think to myself there's nothing better."

And who's to say there is?

Logistics

Phone: (706) 647-9405

Where: Located two blocks off the town square in Thomaston, Georgia at 505 Stewart Avenue. Call Brenda anytime for directions.

Website: www.atimeremembered.net

Prices: Brenda offers four tea times including afternoon, light afternoon, full afternoon, and high tea. Afternoon tea is the least expensive at $5.95 a person plus tax and gratuity, whereas High Tea served Thursday evenings with candlelight dining is a bit pricier at $21.95 per person.

Flannery's Home

Barns outback

Andalusia Home of Flannery O'Conner

When you drive down highway 441 in Milledgeville you will find yourself in the heart of American capitalism. Fast food restaurants, car dealerships, and Wal-Mart line the road, but look closely, it's easy to pass up a very unassuming gravel driveway. Follow that driveway and you will find the home of a woman who sits at the heart of the American Literary world—Flannery O' Conner.

Flannery began her life in Savannah, Georgia. But the author that lives in history lived on a dairy farm from 1951 until her death in 1964. But I might be getting ahead of myself. The man who brought Flannery to life for me met me on a Tuesday afternoon on the farm. Craig Amason is with the Flannery foundation and he has a passion for Flannery's legacy. We spent the afternoon much like Flannery would have spent time on Andalusia sitting on the southern front porch in white high backed rockers talking and that's where Craig condensed Flannery's life.

"Flannery and her mother moved to Milledgeville in 1938," he explained. But they didn't live on the farm. While her Dad worked in

Milledgeville the writer and her mom lived in an apartment downtown. Flannery's Uncle, (her mother's brother) bought the property in the early 1930s. How Flannery and her mom wound up on the farm all has to do with what eventually killed the writer. Now keep in mind that Flannery's dad died from lupus in 1941. In 1950, Flannery came home for a visit but got sick. Doctors found out she too had lupus. "In 1951 she moved to Andalusia, she stayed here because it became apparent she would need some care," explained Craig. The disease did rob her of her energy and she relied on crutches to get around. You can still see the metal walkers in her room.

So while her Mom ran the 543-acre farm, Flannery worked on her writings. Even though her two novels and collection of short stories gained national attention some folks in Central Georgia still don't know about this literary giant's simple surroundings.

"To people around here it's just like an old dairy farm," said Craig. "But when people from this town go abroad to say Italy and say they're from Milledgeville foreigners will say "Oh yeah, Flannery O' Conner." Out of town visitors come here because of their fascination with Flannery O' Conner's fiction and her life, the locals are curious about the property because it's been closed so long."

Flannery's mom left the farm when her daughter died, so everything pretty much stood still until her own death in 1995. When you drive down the driveway you're flanked by rolling green fields. The huge white farmhouse built in the 1850s is the mainstay of the property. Flannery's room is just to the left when you walk inside the front door. She typically spent her mornings writing in her room. Her single bed sits facing a row of glass covered wooden bookshelves. There is a black manual typewriter on a table (Craig says it's not the typewriter Flannery used but it they did find it in the house). It's easy to imagine the young woman working in these surroundings. Craig says it's close to form with a few exceptions, namely its neatness. "Flannery would have had papers and books everywhere."

Right behind the house sits a water tower and a red barn-like building that the family probably used as a parking garage. Flannery also kept bird runs jetting off the sides of the barn. She loved peacocks, ducks, and anything in the aviary family. Farther back sits a hill house and a massive two story rustic looking barn that housed the cow stock. It's a peaceful place and with any kind of an imagination you can see Flannery working off its beauty, charm, and simpleness and therein lies the key to your visit. "It allows them to walk back into 1964 to see what Flannery saw. People go to these literary landmarks to see where an author lived because that's their inspiration. When you read Flannery's stories the farmhouse is in there. This has the potential to be one of the most important literary landmarks in the country."

That of course is for the scholars to work out, but you might want to go to Andalusia so you'll know what everyone else is talking about in Italy!

Logistics

Directions: From Macon take highway 49 into Milledgeville. Hang a left onto Columbia Street (It's a block before Georgia College & State University). Follow Columbia through town passing all the fast food joints. The Andalusia driveway is directly across from the Ramada Inn.

Hours: The farm is open Tuesdays, 10 a.m.–2 p.m. On the third Saturday of the month you can hop on a trolley tour that begins at the Milledgeville Convention and Visitors Bureau at 11 a.m. It's about an hour-long trip. They also give tours by appointment.

Fees: Five dollars to tour Andalusia. They hope to open up more of the house and bring cows and peacocks to the farm.

Website: www.andalusiafarm.org,

Phone: (478) 454-4029

Lee Ward Jr. and
his buddy PJ

Thumper getting ready to race down the track

Elko Mud Boggin

In some Georgia social circles it seems offensive for you to call someone a redneck. That's not true in Elko. The one-horse or maybe we should say one-engine town is mighty proud of the term. As a matter of fact the saying around these parts goes something like this. "If heaven ain't like Elko I don't want to go." Even the concession stand is run by the Rednecks on Tour!

You see Elko plays host to a favorite redneck pastime—mud boggin. For those of you not familiar with the sport, it's a very generic street racing event with a Georgia twist. Drivers race, or in some instances slide and slip, down a 185-foot track that's thick and laden down with pure Georgia red clay. The average run only lasts between four and six seconds!

It's an event that includes the spectators in a very special way. When the engines start roaring and the mud goes a-flyin' the fun shifts into high gear. "They get sprayed and they love it. They think that's cool." Hazel Kersey is a spunky, cowboy hat-wearin', beer-toting woman who helps run things. Her Dad started the event and now the whole family pitches in to help on Saturday nights. "People like it because it's just like NASCAR. They're waiting to see somebody wreck and some do. They go end over end, then the crowd won't breathe, then the driver crawls out, and everyone yells."

This all started when a pond on the property got out of hand twelve years ago. Steve Wiley and his buddies said, "We were sponsoring a softball party one night and some of the boys had four wheel drives and that's how it all started with a pond that didn't hold water." The pond that doesn't hold water is still washing through with enough goo to keep the drivers entertained. In fact Elko is one of the oldest boggins in the state and the US. The first weekend of every month hundreds of folks pile in on the property.

Now even though the scene is right out of a Redneck bible with plenty of coolers, blaring country music, dogs and women with their men sitting in the back of pickup trucks, don't think the racers come in on jalopies. Far from it. "A lot of these guys have 30 and 40 thousand dollars into these cars," Hazel said. The cars roll up to the starting line with names like "Mud Thumper" and "Radio Flyer."

Tony Norrell is a fireman who helps check the safety on the track and make sure the drivers have their helmets strapped on and the roll bars in place. But the guy also races with a six cylinder Ford F-150 equipped with 47-inch tires and emergency flashing lights on top. "This all started out to see who had the baddest street truck. Now it's the fastest," he explained.

The fast fireman took me for a run down the track and it is a different experience staring down the run flanked by all kinds of people waiting to see what you've got. After a few seconds of revving the engine (I'm not sure if this is a technical procedure or just a crowd pleaser) we jolted forward. Tony looked like a man possessed as he worked the steering wheel trying to harness the speed while the earth seeped all around his tires. "Well you've got to get in good hand position, you will not really steer or you'll wind upside down because the ruts will run you." We made it in six seconds. I think he slowed down by a second or two because of my concerns on the flipping issue, but he seemed happy. "It's just an adrenaline rush."

The drivers do get a prize check, just enough to maybe buy some spark plugs and some high octane fuel. That's okay because you get the feeling that even though those NASCAR guys race for millions, mud boggin captures the spirit of the good ole racing days when reputation meant just as much as the money.

Logistics

When: First Saturday of every month. December is Christmas Boggin. Santa makes an appearance and a portion of the money goes to kids' charities.

Cost: $8 to get in the gates. On race day the place opens up about 2:30 in the afternoon. Racing gets going around seven. It will run racers $35 for two runs down the track. There is no extra charge to spend the night on the grounds.

Website: www.elkoboggin.net

Phone: (478) 987-0865

Directions: From Macon go south on I-75 to exit 127. That's the Montezuma/Hawkinsville exit. Hang a left and it's about five miles down the road. Just follow the trucks and the tail lights!

House nestled
under the trees

Crist and Edna on their front porch

The White House Farm Bed and Breakfast

There is always something special about spending the night in a bed and breakfast. But a place in Montezuma takes the uniqueness one step farther by offering you a room on a working dairy farm in the heart of a Mennonite community. Crist Yoder grew up on the 250 acres of land. As a boy his family came to the area when he was two. "In Norfolk, Virginia the land was getting expensive, 18-20 families moved to Georgia. That made me kin to everyone around here," he said smiling. Now about 100 Mennonite families call Montezuma home.

Crist and his wife Edna raised five kids, then a couple of years ago they set to fixing up the place. "Well I always wanted a restaurant, and my wife loves to bake and she's a good cooker!"

The Yoder's had space and the kids were growing up and moving out. "As Mennonite's we always try to have extra room too because people travel through. If our friends had to go to town and stay in a hotel we'd feel bad, Edna said she'd love a bed and breakfast and I could take the repairs off my taxes!"

So they opened up their house, their kitchen, and their hearts to people stopping by. But you'll share the yard with a snoozing cat, a curious lumbering dog named Bear, a good many chickens, pheasants, and the occasional goats and turkeys walking by. It all fits on the farm. At night you might get lucky enough to see a gorgeous sunset dipping over the silo. The tall structure sits next to the barn where the cows come in to feed and give you those stares that only curious cows can claim. I did say this is a working farm, so if you come from the city and want to live the life of a farmer, Crist will take you along, but the morning wake-up call comes early. "We milk at three and three." That's three in the morning and three in the afternoon, of course nowadays machines do most of the yanking on the udders. But the family doesn't serve their main product on the table because it hasn't gone through pasteurization. But what Edna does serve comes right out of the "wow" category. "I like to cook stuffed French toast with cream cheese and raspberry filling, banana nut muffins, sausage hash brown bakes, and cream cheese croissants," said Edna. Crist chimed in, "Anything dairy we push it!"

But they don't push their beliefs. Granted if you stay here you will get a taste of the Mennonite life. They ask you bring well-behaved children and the rooms don't come with televisions. That's because Mennonites don't watch daily TV. "We live by the King James version of the bible," said Crist. "No drinking, no smoking, no divorce or remarriage. We also don't go for this women's lib, I don't know how you feel about it but this is how we feel, it's a man's job to provide the living." Strong statements, but that's the beauty of sitting on the tranquil back porch overlooking masses of green fields and talking to the Yoder's. They don't judge other folks' way of life, they just really believe in their own. Crist says people always ask questions about how the Mennonites live, and that's okay. "People will say, 'well I'm kind of embarrassed to ask,' and I say, 'the only dumb question is the one you don't ask.'"

It's fascinating conversation and on the night I stopped by, the Yoder's had visitors from Belgium. In the dusk of the night we all talked about some of the weightier issues in society, things that seem so far distant with a picturesque backdrop. The Belgians believe they'll come back. "It's the first time we come somewhere and it's so quiet," said Agnes Steenssens. "It's marvelous, every detail is looked at and we like this," added Gilbert Panis.

And the Yoder's like it too. The simple people trade tales with guests from all over the world and some in their own backyard. Crist sums it up best. "It's a completely different breed of people that come. They just want to wander their way through the countryside and we just plum enjoy it!"

Logistics

Phone: (478) 472-7942, **Cell:** (478) 957-6363

Directions: From Macon take I-75 to exit 127. Take a right off the ramp heading towards Montezuma. Motor on down the road about thirteen miles. You'll see the Mennonite restaurant on your left. Just past the Deitsch Haus take a right on White House road. Go about a mile and three quarters to the second stop sign and the Yoder's driveway will stare right back at you.

Prices: At the time of this writing, a single room runs $60, a double is $70. You can get a discount for booking two rooms. Rose, spring bouquet, and magnolia decorate the three rooms.

Website: www.whitehousefarmbnb.com

Extra's: While you're at the bed and breakfast or if you just want to experience some wonderful Mennonite food check out the Deitsch Haus Restaurant. Along with hearty portions of home cooking you can also take home fresh bread and other goodies from the bakery. The adjoining gift shop sells handmade quilts and cannings from the kitchen like jellies, syrups, and relishes.

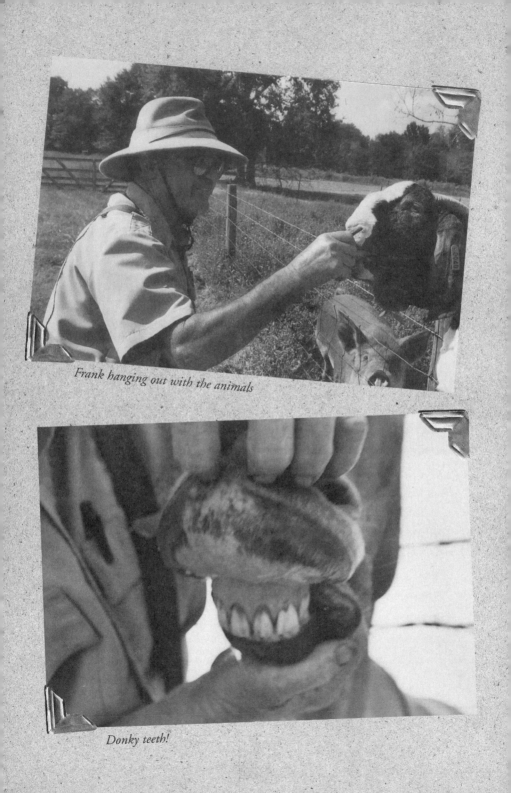

Frank hanging out with the animals

Donky teeth!

Country Vittles

J ust saying the name Country Vittles makes the corners
of your mouth turn up. Go ahead and try it, nobody is
looking! You'll have just as much fun touring the place.
Frank and Betty Lou Ussery have re-created farm life inside
the city limits of Kathleen. They have 17 acres; they farm about
six of it. The two will soon celebrate fifty years of marriage. She's
a retired LPN and he retired from Robins Air Force Base as a Jet
Engine specialist. Frank still loves to tinker and come up with
inventions; he'll talk about his patented Super Duster as much as
he'll share gardening tips for your tomatoes. Listen to what the
guy says, after all he's raised rows of sweet corn, bushels of
cucumbers, squash watermelons, cantaloupe, okra peppers and
more. You can pick your own muscodines, scuppernongs, turnips,
and other farm products when they come into season. The Farm
Bureau of Georgia lists the couple in their Georgia Certified
Market brochures. Frank says he never expected to branch out so
much on the land. "It just kind of evolved into this, my daughter

had little kids in Sunday school class so I would take them on Jeep runs. Then my daughter started working at Perdue Elementary school and she wanted to bring her class out, then all of Houston county wanted to come on out." You can't blame them, the place is beautiful, with big butterfly bushes, donkeys baying in the background, and a huge pig stretched out and sleeping in the sun. It's the sort of atmosphere you can just soak in and enjoy. "The last time I was here the donkey was loud, he just kept going, hee haw!" Mary Shelnutt and her friend Betty Hancock stopped by to pick muscodines in September. "We're widow ladies and we just travel around" said Betty. Betty matter of factly told her friend they'd be back for sweet potatoes and greens in a couple of weeks, but in the middle of all that picking they might just take some time out. "I just wanted to come out and sit under the shade of the trees, it's so peaceful quiet and relaxing." That's how adults see it, kids have a different view of it as they climb into red, white, and blue bucket seat tub-like trains and set out for the grand tour.

"Well we go down into the woods and I show them what poison ivy, honeysuckle and sassafras trees look like. We also see deer. Then whatever we have in season like watermelon, we'll go to the patch pick one and slice it up" explained Frank. Does life get any better for a kid? Yes it does. "I tell them to save the rinds to feed to the donkeys. I got one that will let you pull his lips back and I tell the kids that's what your mouth will look like if you don't brush." Frank said with a farmer's twinkle in his eye.

Betty is quick to offer you a cool glass of lemonade when she's not whipping up concoctions in the kitchen like pepper jelly. "It goes well over cream cheese and crackers." From their kitchen Betty's got a beautiful view of the couple's naturally spring-fed pond. "Sometimes Betty will go out with some tackle and catch three or four nice catfish and we'll have them for dinner." You can do the same, for fifteen dollars you get plump worms and a strong pole to sit under the weeping willows and try your luck—actually it doesn't take much luck. "I keep it stocked with spring catfish and Georgia hybrid brim. I want to make sure they get their money's worth. If they're not biting I give them an extra thirty minutes to catch fish!"

Whether you want the scales or some swaying-in-the-wind sugarcane stop by Country Vittles. Frank and Betty would be happy to show you some good ole farm like hospitality.

Logistics

Phone: (478) 987-3331

Directions: Take I-75 from Macon to Exit 138. Take a left traveling east. Go to the second red light and hang a left on Houston Lake Road. When you see the dam on your left take a right on Bear Branch Road. Take another left on Farr Road (it's a little ways down). The Ussery's live at 173 Farr Road and they do have a Georgia Certified Farm Market sign outside.

Email: countryvittles@aol.com

Reservations are required for official tours, but if you're just stopping in to buy veggies a look around is free. Field trips, which include fishing, cost $5 per person with a minimum of $100 fee per visiting group. Fishing will run you $15 for two hours of dropping your pole in the water and yanking out fish.

Zena looking for attention

Celia working on a project

A Touch of Glass
Stained Glass Studio

S tained glass making is a magical kind of art. One
gallery in Forsyth wants you to enjoy the final pieces
but they've also put out an invitation for you to see
how it's all done.

Celia Meech-Hennigan and her husband own A Touch
of Glass studio and an adjoining art gallery called Studio 51.
Her passion lies within the colored pieces she brings to life
and unlike other galleries; this one comes with a very
personal tour.

"It's like an art appreciation class," explained Celia.
"What I love is the idea of educating people. If you give
someone a price on the phone they say Whoa, but when
they walk through here they say, is this all it costs?"

Stained glass commissioned pieces and restoration work
can get pricey, but it's very labor intensive. If you take the

tour you'll start out with a video set in France. France is where doctors brought Celia into the world and she loves the European influence. On the tape you'll learn how the glass is split and the color is added. "They see everything the glass goes through before I get it, so when they come in they don't say 'how did you get that design?'" Then it's off to explore the day in and day out life of an artist. Besides Celia you will have a special ambassador by your side for the adventure. Zena is the studio mascot, the lumbering English Mastiff shuffles through the place, that's when she's not on her back purring like a cat and waiting for you to rub her massive belly. "She's definitely a highlight, one day I noticed one lady had her shoe off and she was swinging her leg, then I noticed she was scratching Zena with her foot!"

Zena is a big dog but that's okay because the building is huge, and laid out over 22-thousand square feet. For years manufacturers used it as a warehouse and it still has that feel of making things happen about the place. Big layout and design tables sit next to windows with daylight streaming in and bouncing off the glass.

"After the tape I show them cutting, fabricating, painting, and mudding or cementing. I do open the kiln so they can see the glass melting. Some of the heat comes out and you see red hot pieces that look like lava." You can bet the pieces in the kiln will show up in someone's living room, restaurant wall or steeple chapel. "We do a lot of restoration and this is a working studio. Most everything you see is produced for paying customers."

The productions sometimes look like puzzles. Stained glass is
beautiful but it doesn't last forever. Celia says after eighty
years or so the lead around the glass wears out just like your
windows at home. So you'll see her staff doing painstaking
meticulous work to make sure everything goes back together
correctly. Some projects resemble massive intricate paint by
numbers designs with the cutouts of sky, hands and faces
sitting off to the side waiting to go back to their ancient
original home.

As you wander through you'll see tools that do the
daintiest of work, to the tougher workhorse materials like
Plaster of Paris and Dremels getting ready to crank out
Celia's latest design. It's really insightful to see how the mind
and hands of artists work, a trip behind the scenes that's
brings as much clarity to the process as the sun shining
through a brilliantly colored piece of glass.

Logistics

Phone: (478) 994-8683
Website: www.atgstudio.com
Directions: 51 West Adams Street, one block off the Forsyth
town square
Cost: Tours run $7.00 a person and Celia says you must
book them in advance! Plan to spend at least an hour
learning and looking around the place. It doesn't cost
anything to go in, look, and shop at Studio 51. It's a typical
gallery with all kinds of atypical artwork for sale.

Photo by Kim Smaha

Thanks for reading *Cotton, Cornbread, and Conversations.*
I hope it leads you to new adventures.
If you come across a new adventure, contact me.
It may wind up in our next book!

Suzanne Lawler
C/o Mercer University Press
1400 Coleman Avenue
Macon, GA 31207